Praise for
★ **Baseball's Leading** *~~Lady~~*

"Andrea Williams brings the Queen of the Negro Leagues back to life through the pages of this wonderfully written and introspective look at the most important woman in baseball history."
—Bob Kendrick, President, Negro Leagues Baseball Museum

"Andrea Williams comes at the reader like a masterful pitcher with a full repertoire at the ready. She weaves the story of the Negro Leagues with a primer on Black history and, most impressive, a case study in the rise and fall of a successful Black-owned business."
—Andrew Maraniss, bestselling author of
Strong Inside* and *Games of Deception

"An important hole in baseball literature is addressed in this nonfiction recollection of businesswoman Effa Manley's role in the rise and fall of the Negro Leagues."
—*School Library Journal*

"A fascinating contribution to baseball and racial history." **—*Kirkus Reviews***

"With a flair for bringing clarity and excitement to back office wheeling and dealing, Williams offers a potent complement to Nelson's *We Are the Ship*."
—*The Bulletin of the Center for Children's Books*

"A well-organized, detailed introduction to Effa Manley." **—*Booklist***

"For middle-school-and-up readers seeking historical role models of resilience." **—*The Seattle Times***

"Well-selected black-and-white photographs—along with the fascinating history—make for an inviting read." **—*The Horn Book***

Baseball's Leading Lady

Effa Manley and the Rise and Fall of the Negro Leagues

Andrea Williams

SQUARE
FISH

Roaring Brook Press
New York

For Alyssa and Alana. May you always see
clearly and speak loudly. –A. W.

SQUARE FISH

An imprint of Macmillan Publishing Group, LLC
120 Broadway, New York, NY 10271 • mackids.com

Our books may be purchased in bulk for promotional, educational, or
business use. Please contact your local bookseller or the Macmillan Corporate
and Premium Sales Department at (800) 221-7945 ext. 5442 or by
email at MacmillanSpecialMarkets@macmillan.com.

Library of Congress Cataloging-in-Publication Data
Names: Williams, Andrea, author.
Title: Baseball's leading lady : Effa Manley and the rise and fall of the Negro Leagues /
Andrea Williams.
Description: | New York : Roaring Brook Press, 2023. | Includes
bibliographical references and index. | Audience: Ages 10–14 | Audience: Grades 4–6 |
Summary: "The true story of Effa Manley, the first and only woman in the Baseball Hall
of Fame, and her ownership role in the Negro Leagues leading up to the integration
of Major League Baseball"—Provided by publisher.
Identifiers: LCCN 2020010677 | ISBN 9781250623720 (hardcover)
Subjects: LCSH: Manley, Effa, 1897–1981—Juvenile literature. | Negro leagues—
History—Juvenile literature. | Baseball—United States—History—Juvenile literature. |
Baseball team owners—United States—Biography—Juvenile literature. | Women
baseball team owners—United States—Biography—Juvenile literature. | African
American women—Biography—Juvenile literature. | Newark Eagles (Baseball team)—
Juvenile literature.
Classification: LCC GV865.M325 W55 2020 | DDC 796.357092 [B]—dc23
LC record available at https://lccn.loc.gov/2020010677

Originally published in the United States by Roaring Brook Press
First Square Fish edition, 2023
Book designed by Mercedes Padró
Square Fish logo designed by Filomena Tuosto
Printed in the United States of America by Lakeside Book Company, Harrisonburg, Virginia

ISBN 978-1-250-86654-7 (paperback)
1 3 5 7 9 10 8 6 4 2

AR: 8.8 / LEXILE: 1300L

CONTENTS

INTRODUCTION

It was 1946 in New York—early fall, September. It was that electric season that bridged the smothering heat of summer and the iciness of winter with brisk mornings and cooler nights, the time when kids were settling into their school-day routines and the baseball games played on diamonds across the country mattered most.

New York was the epicenter of America's pastime then, and there were enough teams around town for every fan to choose their favorite. Some followed the New York Giants and their right fielder, Mel Ott, the pure power hitter who led his team in home runs for eighteen consecutive seasons—a record that's yet to be broken. Others flocked to the legendary Ebbets Field to see the Brooklyn Dodgers take on the St. Louis Cardinals, the Chicago Cubs, and the crosstown Giants, too. Others, still, pledged allegiance to the

New York Yankees, with their pinstripes signifying a team that was all business, all the time, and their ten World Series championships from 1923 to 1943 the indisputable proof.

But on September 17, 1946, the biggest, most important baseball game in New York didn't feature Yogi Berra or the Babe. That evening, it was Black baseball's finest on display. The Negro American League's Kansas City Monarchs and the Negro National League's Newark Eagles were facing off at the Polo Grounds in Upper Manhattan for Game 1 of the Negro World Series. So while the Polo Grounds usually featured the hometown Giants, Ott and

On September 17, 1946, more than nineteen thousand fans gathered in New York's Polo Grounds stadium to see the Newark Eagles face off against the Kansas City Monarchs in Game 1 of the Negro World Series.

his teammates had given way to the Monarchs' Satchel Paige and Hilton Smith, along with the Eagles' Larry Doby and Monte Irvin.

✳✳✳

From her seat in the owner's box, Effa Manley surveyed the crowd of Black and brown fans. The men wore three-piece suits, the women, veiled fascinators and wide-brimmed hats. All were clad in their Sunday best, and Effa was dressed to the nines, too. Black baseball games were always an occasion—the rare family-friendly event on the social calendar—but this game was even more special. Through twelve seasons of uncertainty, on and off the field, this moment was Effa's wildest dreams come true.

Effa turned her attention to the diamond, to her Eagles scattered around the dirt and grass during warm-ups. They were a glorious-looking crew, classy and handsome, and they would look even better during Game 2 at Ruppert Stadium. Then they'd be clad in their bright white uniforms so new that the flannel of the jerseys would still be crisp and firm against their skin.

Abe, Effa's husband and co-owner of the Eagles, had been surprised when she decided to purchase the uniforms for a staggering $700. Normally, player uniforms had to be unraveling at the seams before Effa would consider replacing them; even then, it was the catcher and pitcher, maybe the infield basemen, who got outfitted. The fans could see them more clearly, she reasoned, so they needed to be the best-dressed on the field. Black baseball may have been operating on a shoestring compared with the white pro teams, but Effa saw no reason for her team to look penniless—even if it sometimes was.

No, there would be no hardship on display during the '46 Negro World Series. If anything, there would be celebration—of Black baseball, of Black community, of new Black money that had come streaming into the community via the war and accompanying hiring sprees. Effa and her Eagles had experienced many lean years, but these prosperous times had made it all worth it.

There were more than nineteen thousand people milling about the stadium that September night, and Effa was thankful for every one. So many of them had been around for years, supporting the team since its inaugural season in 1935, back when a Negro World Series was unfathomable. Now they were there to witness history.

Back on the field, Leon Day, the Eagles' star pitcher, tossed balls to catcher Biz Mackey while Effa watched silently. A Newark victory was close—*so* close that Effa could feel it. Yet even as her chest swelled with pride and possibility, she couldn't shake the worry that gathered in the corners of her mind.

No matter the jubilation that surrounded her, Effa knew that the future of the Eagles—the future of all of Negro Leagues Baseball, in fact—was in jeopardy.

✳✳✳

By the time that first game of the 1946 Negro World Series rolled around, Effa had already spent years on the battlefield for Black baseball. She'd confronted Branch Rickey when he signed Jackie Robinson without paying the Kansas City Monarchs for his contract—and that was before he had the nerve to pilfer one of her own Eagles players. She'd argued with other owners of Black baseball teams, pleading with them to tighten up their business affairs for respectability's sake. She'd even challenged Black sportswriters who advocated for baseball's integration without considering the real, lasting effect it would have on the Negro Leagues.

Effa loved baseball, to be sure, but it was more than just the crack of the bat and the thrill of triumph that drew her to the game. She saw the Negro Leagues as a vehicle to transport the Black community to a position of equality in American society, to provide jobs and financial stability where they were sorely lacking, and to give Black boys and girls regular opportunities to witness victory when so much of their lives was mired in defeat.

That Effa was a successful team owner and league executive in the highly competitive world of professional baseball is laudable. That she was successful as a Black woman in the 1930s and '40s, when gender discrimination hung like a heavy harness around the necks of *all* women, is extraordinary. Still, Effa didn't draw attention to her otherness; she didn't flaunt her pioneering efforts in meetings or press conferences. Most of the time, if asked, she credited her husband for her achievements. That was the socially acceptable way to handle things back then, to be sure, but Effa also had other reasons for shifting attention away from her groundbreaking presence in professional baseball, even when others chose to focus on it. Namely, she was busy.

Effa had games to win.

* * *

Eagles ace Leon Day was shaky from the very start of Game 1 between Newark and Kansas City, allowing the Monarchs to score their first run in the top of the opening inning. And despite having five players who hit above .300 during the regular season, the Eagles couldn't counter with a run of their own in the bottom of the first. Meanwhile, Hilton Smith, Kansas City's starting pitcher, was near perfect. He held the Eagles scoreless for five innings, but

Smith's reliable arm began to waver after the fifth inning, and after walking Larry Doby to lead off the sixth, his teammate, the legendary Satchel Paige, was brought in for relief. It was like trading a tornado for a hurricane.

As soon as he took the mound, Paige struck out Eagles utility player Monte Irvin and first baseman Lennie Pearson. Doby did manage to steal second base, but with two outs, Effa still had cause for concern. Even though the Eagles were playing less than thirty miles away from Newark, at the supposedly neutral Polo Grounds, they hadn't been able to leverage their near home-field advantage to get on top.

But then: hope!

Doby, the quiet second baseman who would later follow Jackie Robinson and become the second Black player in the Majors, scored on a single from outfielder Johnny Davis that smacked into the right-field wall.

Just like that, the score was tied at 1, and Effa's team was right back in the game.

When the Eagles went back on defense in the top of the seventh, the crowd was enraptured, the cheers deafening. This was the Eagles' opportunity. If they could keep the mighty Monarchs scoreless for the next three innings, Newark might be able to secure a victory after all.

But Satchel Paige refused to stop fighting! He'd already proven his dominance on the mound, and when he stepped up to the plate in the seventh inning, he showed that he could also answer Newark's comeback with his bat. Paige hit the ball up the middle of the infield, where it careened off the glove of Eagles relief pitcher Rufus Lewis for a single. Then, when Doby fielded the ball, he overthrew first base on the attempted putout, allowing Paige to advance to second.

With another Monarchs player in scoring position, Effa was once again worrying, hoping, praying...

But in the end, her prayers weren't enough.

Herb Souell, the Monarchs' third baseman, singled to left field, and Paige coasted home, pushing the team from Kansas City back into the lead. The score was 2–1, and it would remain that way through the eighth and ninth innings, sending Effa and her Eagles back to Newark down one game in the series.

✳✳✳

Effa took a loss as hard as any man in baseball. She thought her boys were the best, and when they failed to meet her incredibly high standards, her emotions came bursting forth like floodwaters from a dam. The loss to the Monarchs was tough, but it wasn't just the score that disappointed Effa. The Eagles were wrapping up their best year in team history, and the defeat felt ominous, like a sign of horrible things to come. The hard-fought game, the too-close score, the win that was just out of reach . . .

It was a stern reminder—the tangible evidence—that no matter how hard she and her team fought, they just might lose after all.

PART I

A Rebel Is Born

COLOR LINES

When Effa Louise Brooks Manley was born in Philadelphia on March 27, 1897, she was thrust into a world obsessed with color.

There was the blue green of the Schuylkill, the river that still snakes its way through southeastern Pennsylvania, ultimately meeting the Delaware River in Philadelphia, the city where Effa was born. There was the slate gray of the smoke plumes that blew from the many factories dotting the skyline, a sign of the town's industrial prowess. And there was the stark white of the snow that fell often in Philly—sometimes even into April, when winter refused to give way to spring.

Mostly, however, the world was concerned with the color of people.

At the turn of the century, with memories of slavery and the Civil War still fresh, America was struggling to come to terms with the promise of freedom that had been made to the formerly enslaved and their descendants. Immediately after the war, progress appeared to be on the horizon. But then, just as quickly as advancement began to sprout through the smothering choke of oppression, it was tamped down, and every painstaking stride was rolled back, one by one.

In the northern part of the country, in and around Effa's urban hometown, Black men and women faced racism that, while less overt, was just as prevalent as what their peers faced in the South. Northern Black people weren't working as sharecroppers on the same plantations where their families had once been enslaved, nor were they fearful of the night-riding KKK. But there was still an overwhelming belief that Black people were inferior, that the advantages afforded to white men and women were never meant to transfer.

Black families in cities like New York, Pittsburgh, and Boston were often forced to live in substandard housing and, in many cases, required to send their children to substandard schools. For adults who could get jobs, the work was menial, underpaid, and devoid of advancement opportunities. Meanwhile, white suffragists abandoned the Black women who had once been their allies, making clear their position that only white women should be given the right to vote.

America's failure to keep its promises to the Black community, and its persistence in affording privileges based on the color of a person's skin, may have been most glaring in the workforce, the education system, and the voting booth. But racism knew no bounds. Its stench was everywhere and permeating all aspects of society, including sports.

Across the country, Black people began to realize that there was no Declaration of Independence for them, that the Emancipation Proclamation did little to guarantee true liberation for those whose skin bore the pigmentation of their African ancestors. Indeed, even as lawmakers passed legislation that governed the military, dictated punishment for crimes, and controlled other aspects of daily life, a different set of rules regulated American race relations. These statutes, both spoken and unspoken, demanded total separation of Black and white, in physical proximity as well as socioeconomic status.

As a young girl just beginning to understand the ways of a segregated world, Effa was still many years from becoming the woman who would lead protests and boycotts, denouncing racism and demanding that Black baseball players and executives be shown the same respect as their white counterparts. But even as a child she knew such rules were ridiculous, and she needed only to look in the mirror for proof.

Effa's mother, Bertha Brooks, was a mulatto woman, meaning she had both Black and white ancestry. Before Effa was born, Bertha had been married to a Black man with whom she birthed four children. A later marriage, to another Black man, resulted in Effa's two younger siblings. In the middle was Effa, her skin noticeably pale next to the deeper hues of her brothers' and sisters'.

Effa's mother was a skilled seamstress who often worked in the homes of white families, sewing everything from common pants and shirts to the fanciest gowns and tuxedos. While employed by a wealthy white stockbroker named John Marcus Bishop, Mrs. Brooks had a sexual encounter with her boss, and Effa's birth was the result. When she arrived, Effa carried the genes of both her mother and father, her very existence an olive-tinted representation of two worlds forbidden from mixing.

***

Effa was in first grade when the principal of Newton Grammar School summoned her, the white woman's voice stern and her face, no doubt, in an angry scowl. "Why are you always with the colored children?" she asked.

Despite an 1881 Pennsylvania State law that outlawed school segregation, and an 1887 equal rights bill that forbade segregation in any public accommodations, most Black and white children were still educated separately. There were some integrated schools, however, including the one that Effa attended. But even when white children and Black children were allowed to attend the same educational institutions, social norms dictated that they keep their distance as much as possible. This confused Effa, as did her principal's anger that she would defy such convention.

Effa considered her fair-skinned hands, her fingers that were the color of pale coastal sand—nearly white, but not quite so. Some of her friends and family had skin that was tan like a field of wheat; some were draped in rich brown hues; others were so dark they were almost black, like the rich, life-giving soil of a lush garden. The differences were obvious, yes, but they were comforting to Effa. Comforting and natural.

Effa's principal disagreed. If Effa was as white as she appeared, she would surely only play with other white children. Or maybe, the principal assumed, Effa's decision to associate with Black children at school meant that she, too, was Black.

As soon as she got home, Effa told her mother about the conversation and the principal's questioning of her choice of friends. Effa was looking for understanding from her mother, perhaps an explanation of why skin color mattered so much in a place as insignificant as the Newton Grammar School playground. Instead, Effa received a response that seemed to complicate matters even more. "You tell that woman you're just as white as she is," her mother said.

Even though Effa's father was white, US Census records show that her mother had at least some Black heritage. Effa was as much her mother's child as she was her father's, of course, but Effa's mother knew that, in a color-crazed world, even one drop of Black blood rendered a person wholly nonwhite. Effa's mother *also* knew that people like Effa—people whose complexions appeared more white than black—had options. They didn't have to follow the world's color lines. They could live between them.

Since the era of slavery, fair-skinned Black people, typically of mixed heritage, had been denouncing their Black heritage and "passing" for white. The lighter a person's skin, the easier it was to disappear into white society, to instantly rise above the lowest rungs of the socioeconomic ladder and enjoy a life that was otherwise unobtainable. Passing came with drawbacks, though, and those who chose that path had to live in utter secrecy, far away from family and friends who knew the truth. For some people, the benefits were worth the cost.

Effa's mother didn't explain these truths. She didn't tell Effa about her worries as a mother raising Black children in a society that resented their existence, nor did she express her desire for Effa to reap at least some of the benefits afforded to her father, her principal, and all the other white folks in Philadelphia. Instead, she snapped, her words just as baffling to Effa as the principal's had been.

Throughout her childhood, Effa's family lived squarely in Philadelphia's Black community. There, they were no different from other Black families who ate at Black-owned restaurants, shopped at Black-owned grocers, attended Black churches, and learned of local happenings from Black newspapers. It was the world Effa knew and loved, and it was the world in which she would choose to remain all her life. Even as she used her light skin to land jobs that were normally reserved for whites and to book rooms in white-only hotels, Effa's heart—and her career—stayed in the Black community.

Nothing that her mother said, or her principal questioned, would ever change that.

FIELDS OF DREAMS

On May 3, 1887, ten years before Effa was born, the *Buffalo Commercial* newspaper of Buffalo, New York, ran a brief report on the preceding day's game between the Newark Little Giants of the International League and the hometown Buffalo Bisons:

> The Newarks scored their second victory from the Bisons yesterday. It was a good game all the way through. Stovey and Walsh were the pitchers, and each was well supported. Walker caught for the Newarks and Callahan for the visitors.

The writer's emphasis on each team's pitcher-catcher combination, otherwise known as the "battery," was common. Of all the positions on the field, those two were considered baseball's most valuable; after all, it was nearly impossible to win without a strong player on the mound and another behind the plate.

With George Stovey, Moses Fleetwood Walker (*pictured*) formed the first all-Black battery in 1887, proving that Black athletes were just as talented as their white counterparts.

George Stovey and Moses Fleetwood Walker were good enough to lead the Newark team to a 4–3 victory over their opponents that day, but that, in itself, doesn't fully speak to the importance of the report. In his brevity, the writer omitted a most significant detail: Stovey and Walker were two Black players on an otherwise all-white team. In fact, they were the first Black battery in the history of professional baseball.

Indeed, while some historians, baseball fans, and members of the general public regard Jackie Robinson as the first Black player to play Major League Baseball, Robinson's career doesn't begin to tell the full history of Black athletes in pro baseball. The four-sport star from UCLA did break modern baseball's color barrier when he signed his first contract with the Brooklyn Dodgers organization in 1945, but many years before that, Black players like Walker and Stovey were already taking the field.

∗∗∗

When the first documented baseball game was played in 1846, between clubs from New York and Brooklyn, the sport was still a novelty. Back then, it's unlikely that anyone would have predicted that baseball would eventually become America's pastime.

During the Civil War, soldiers engaged in informal contests to keep their spirits up and their minds off the battle, all the while raising the profile of the country's new sport. Many of those men played baseball after the war, too, both as recreation and as entertainment for a growing fan base. As a result, the game continued to increase in popularity, quickly spreading into the civilian world, where white and Black players took the field.

Baseball was being played throughout the country by the mid-1880s, but the northeastern United States was its de facto headquarters. In New York, DC, and elsewhere, teams of all races began taking shape, but it was Philadelphia—the city that birthed Effa Manley, future queen of the Negro Leagues—that became one of the most active incubators for Black baseball. And of all the men pushing Philly's Black baseball scene to the forefront, no one was more powerful than Octavius Catto.

In Philadelphia, Octavius Catto established himself as both a leader in Black baseball circles and a vocal advocate for Black civil rights.

Catto was an affluent, well-educated member of Philadelphia's Black elite, as well as a staunch abolitionist who had been free during the era of slavery. He enlisted in the Civil War as a member of the all-Black Fifth Brigade and saw how tough the war was on Black soldiers in particular. Black soldiers received lower pay than their white counterparts and often faced attacks from white civilians, but Catto welcomed the opportunity to fight for his country nonetheless.

He wanted to support the antislavery cause and help the Union rise victorious. Like many white soldiers, he also learned to play baseball.

After the war's end, Catto continued to work for Black advancement, and with baseball becoming an increasingly popular—and more lucrative—endeavor, he saw the sport as yet another vehicle to propel his people toward progress. He organized the Pythian Base Ball Club of Philadelphia in 1866 with this in mind, and in a relatively short time, his team was among the best in all of Black baseball.

The Pythians won 90 percent of games played against other Black teams in Philadelphia, New York, Baltimore, and Washington, DC. So talented and well run was Catto's organization that even the *Sunday Mercury*, a white Philadelphia newspaper, referred to the team as "our fellows" when reporting a game between the Pythians and the Alert Base Ball Club of DC.

Yet despite some white support, the Pythians faced a harsh reality as an all-Black team. Philadelphia was more accepting of Black people than other cities—certainly more so than neighboring baseball communities like Baltimore, Maryland, and Richmond, Virginia, where slavery had flourished only a few years prior—but the racial barriers were still there. Catto's club, which could not lease or own its own grounds, or play games at several segregated fields across the city, suffered from a lack of access that would plague Black baseball teams well into the next century. The Pythians followed the social expectations of the time—always deferring to whites, always effusive in thanks—but it was never enough.

In their most devastating confrontation with the realities of American race relations, Catto's Pythians were denied membership in the National Association of Base Ball Players (NABBP), baseball's first governing body. The NABBP was founded in 1858 to provide support for the growing number of players, and while no initial rule forbade Black teams from joining, the association added a key clause to its constitution after Catto applied in 1867:

> *It is not presumed by your (nominating) committee that any clubs who have applied are composed of persons of color, or any portion of them; … and they unanimously report against the admission of any club which may be composed of one or more colored persons.*

The country was knee-deep in Reconstruction efforts then, with Northern and Southern whites still struggling to reconcile in the aftermath of the country's bloodiest war. On one hand, Americans seemed to clamor for unity; on the other, uniting North and South took precedence over the unification of Black and white.

In *The Negro Leagues, 1869–1960*, baseball historian and author Leslie Heaphy writes:

> *Some baseball leadership wanted to use the game as a way to ameliorate existing sectional hostility left from the war. If baseball could help bring white northerners and southerners together as reconstruction was slowly being abandoned, then this would be encouraged. If that meant casting aside Black players for the time being, that's what would be done.*

The clause in the NABBP constitution represented the first—and only—time a written rule actually barred Black players from organized baseball. When the NABBP reorganized as the National Association of Professional Base Ball Players in 1871, four years after Catto's application, this clause was not included in official documents. But it didn't matter. The seed of exclusion had already been planted, and it was quickly growing roots.

Tragically, 1871 also marked the year of Catto's death. Though Black men had been granted the right to vote via the Fifteenth Amendment, which was ratified on February 3, 1870, exercising that right was extremely difficult—even dangerous. The white supremacist KKK was most active in the South, where members regularly terrorized Black voters, but Northern states like Pennsylvania were likewise rife with whites who were known to attack Black men in an effort to keep them from the polls.

Despite these risks, Catto was committed to voting—he simply purchased a gun to protect himself. Unfortunately, Catto was never able to fire that gun before he was shot several times while en route to the polls on October 10, 1871. He later died from his wounds.

Catto's Pythians folded after his murder, but individuals from the team, as well as many other Black players, continued to play baseball. Their talents opened doors, earning them positions on predominantly white teams whose managers valued win-loss records more than de facto segregation. This practice would continue for nearly two decades until, sadly, those brave individuals would be forced out, too.

✳✳✳

A few hours north of Philadelphia, in Binghamton, New York, John "Bud" Fowler made his own mark on Black baseball. He started his career in 1878 and played in 465 games over ten years; he's also the first Black player to join a team that was considered professional, not amateur or semipro. Fowler joined the Binghamton team of the International League in 1887 and was a clear offensive force, hitting .350 that year. But Binghamton released him midseason when Fowler's own teammates threatened to quit if he and another Black Binghamton player remained on the team.

There were other early Black baseball stars, too—men like Sol White, whose *Official Base Ball Guide* became a preeminent handbook on the history of early baseball, and Frank Grant, a middle infielder with great throwing range and a quick bat. But of all those courageous athletes who broke barriers in sports and society in the late nineteenth century, Moses Fleetwood Walker is perhaps the most well known.

While Fowler had been the first Black player to play on a professional team, Fleet took those pioneering efforts one step further by becoming the first Black player on a Major League team when he suited up with the Toledo Blue Stockings of the American Association in 1884. (This was Fleet's second year with the Blue Stockings, but the team played minor-league ball in 1883.) Joining Fleet on the roster was his brother, Weldy, though

Weldy played only a handful of games in 1884—and never when Fleet was in the lineup.

It is unclear whether the brothers' skin color affected their manager's decision to avoid playing them at the same time, but the racism they endured throughout their careers was unmistakable. In 1919, decades after Fleet's time with the Blue Stockings, Toledo pitcher Tony Mullane revealed how he'd felt about having Fleet on his team:

> *I had it in for him. He was the best catcher I ever worked with, but I disliked a Negro and whenever I had to pitch to him I used to pitch anything I wanted without looking at his signals.*

In 1887, the same year Fowler was forced out of the International League midseason, matters of race came to a head for Fleet and every other professional Black player. On July 14, just two months after he joined the Newark Little Giants and partnered with George Stovey to produce the first all-Black pitcher-catcher duo, Fleet Walker crossed paths with Cap Anson of the Chicago White Stockings.

Rather, they *almost* crossed paths.

The matchup never materialized, as Anson refused to take the field if either Fleet or Stovey suited up for the Newark Little Giants.

Anson was one of the most popular players of the era, and he didn't hesitate to exert his influence. In fact, this wasn't the first time the first baseman had voiced his racist views. He'd objected to playing against Fleet four years prior, when Fleet was still playing with Toledo; unfortunately for Anson, the Northwestern League had ruled that Fleet could play. While Anson had the option to walk away, he knew he'd have to give up his day's salary if he did.

An angry Anson joined his team on the field in 1883, but not before declaring he wouldn't "play no more with the n——r in." And he never had to. Just before the 1887 game between the White Stockings and the Newark team, Anson put his foot down once again. This time—thanks to Anson's increased clout, as well as both owners' unwillingness to forfeit—neither Stovey nor Fleet played. What's more, the International League, of which the Newark Little Giants was a member, voted later that day to ban the signing of any additional Black players.

There were no Black players in the Majors at the time of this decision, and once the Black minor-league players, including Fleet, finished out their contracts, no others would be allowed in for nearly sixty years.

Anson's stance became the crux of a so-called gentleman's agreement—so-called not because there was anything "gentlemanly" about it, but because it was never decreed by written rule. Yet even as the agreement remained unwritten, it became all-powerful, the hidden force that would guide the evolution of professional baseball for generations to come.

STRONG ARMS

Black players may have been forced out of white baseball in 1887, but that didn't stop them from forming their own teams and continuing to play. Across the country, enterprising men formed independent teams that traveled the country, going head-to-head against other independent teams while continuing to prove that Black athletes had as much of a right to take the field as anyone else. In the spirit of Octavius Catto, these men saw baseball as an opportunity to make money as well as racial progress.

Like white baseball, Black baseball had its dominant teams and superstar players, and one, in particular, would extend the legacies of Catto, Moses Fleetwood Walker, and George Stovey, taking

Black ball even further than they dreamed it could go. Andrew "Rube" Foster became a star because of his unparalleled pitching, but his advocacy for Black players and his efforts to organize Black baseball would make him an icon.

✳ ✳ ✳

Born in 1879 in Calvert, Texas, Foster took to the baseball diamond quickly and began pitching with the Waco Yellow Jackets after finishing eighth grade. With limited income-earning prospects for Black men in the Deep South, making a living as a baseball player seemed the most promising plan for the talented Foster, so he left

his home state in 1902 to join the all-Black Chicago Union Giants. The team was led by Frank Leland, an accomplished player who's better known as a pioneering manager in early Black baseball.

Though Foster had been paid to play with Waco, he made far less

Standing at over six feet tall and more than two hundred pounds, Rube Foster was one of the most dominant pitchers in baseball in the early 1900s.

than what he could earn with the Union Giants. Black baseball teams were all independent then, so each club was responsible for generating its own income, primarily by scheduling games against other teams. In a practice known as *barnstorming*, teams spent days and weeks on the road, traveling anywhere they could find a willing opponent. Playing against another club with a few loyal followers was good, but playing against a team with a large and well-established fan base was even better because more fans meant more revenue.

Like the Yellow Jackets, the Union Giants were an independent, barnstorming club, but being based in Chicago gave the team regular access to much bigger crowds than a team playing in tiny Waco, Texas. As a result, there were much bigger profits to split among players.

Because he joined the lineup only to pinch-hit, Foster's first appearance for the Union Giants was less than extraordinary. He more than made up for it, however, when he finally took the mound a few days later. Over the next three months, Foster lost only one game; according to some historians, he also earned the nickname that he would carry the rest of his life.

In an exhibition game against an all-white team played after Major League Baseball's regular season ended, Foster triumphed over the Philadelphia Athletics' Rube Waddell, a pitcher who would go on to lead the American League in strikeouts for six straight seasons. With baseball divided along color lines, a common way to describe a Black player's prowess was to compare him to a well-known white player. So after beating one of the best hurlers in organized white baseball, Foster is believed to have been given his opponent's name, Rube, as his new moniker.

Indeed, Foster was so talented that even white newspapers, which rarely discussed matters that were central to the Black community, covered his exploits. In 1907, Frederic North Shorey of Chicago's *Inter-Ocean* newspaper wrote a sweeping profile of the star pitcher. His writing was blatantly racist and included a comparison of Foster to a "typical stage darky," but it also gushed over the player's greatness:

> *When he enters the box he takes a calm survey of the field to see that his men are in place, sizes up the batter, and suddenly, before the batter realizes what has happened, the ball is over the plate for one strike. This is the most frequent of [Rube's] tricks, and he has plenty of them. He has the faculty of whipping the ball across the plate with or without*

the preliminary winding up which is the most painful per-
formance of so many pitchers, and he can do it underhand,
with a sidewheel motion, overhand, or apparently snap it
with his wrist. And when he is in a tight place he seemingly
can pitch so that the ball will be batted to a certain place.

Not surprisingly, Foster's arm was highly recruited, and he moved around quite often, pitching short stints for a handful of independent teams when the offer was right. Foster left Chicago to join the Philadelphia Giants for the 1906 season, and although a dispute with the Giants' manager over salaries quickly ended his tenure with the team, it also solidified his mission to advocate on behalf of Black players.

In 1907, Foster rejoined his Chicago team, which had recently been renamed the Leland Giants. In addition to reclaiming his position atop the pitcher's mound, the exacting Foster also became player-manager of the team, making his first legacy-defining step toward Black baseball's executive ranks.

It was relatively common for a veteran player to coach his team on the field while also holding a spot on the roster, but

Foster's position was particularly unique. He took over the team's bookings and secured a 40 percent cut of ticket sales, also known as gate receipts, for the players. This arrangement resulted in greater personal profits for Foster, while also giving him a role in the team's overall business decisions.

On the field, Foster led the Giants to their best season ever, while, off the field, he ensured that higher team revenue translated into better player benefits, including guaranteed salaries. No longer driven only by wins and losses, Foster had officially launched his self-imposed mission to learn the business of baseball and improve the fortunes of all Black players.

The Giants quickly became a marquee attraction in Chicago and surrounding areas, but Foster's vision for transforming Black baseball extended well beyond the Midwest. Unfortunately, his time in Philadelphia had shown him that Black teams on the East Coast faced a unique, and extraordinary, challenge.

His name was Nat Strong.

✳✳✳

On the Eastern Seaboard, Nat Strong was Foster's closest contemporary—a man with shrewd business sense and a vision for Black baseball as big business. But Strong was a booking agent, not an athlete, and unlike Foster, he wasn't concerned about the overall well-being of Black teams and players. For Strong, profit was the primary motivator, and despite his blond hair and blue eyes, he held a firm grip on much of New England's Black baseball market. In fact, he was likely the most powerful booking agent there was, at one point controlling the schedules of more than a dozen Black teams, including the Cuban Stars, New York Black Yankees, and Brooklyn Royal Giants.

By the early 1900s, Strong owned two semi-pro teams in New York and had considerable baseball contacts throughout the city, as well as political ties that gave him access to many of the city's ballparks. In 1907, the same year Foster took an active role in the Giants'

Nat Strong was a powerful booking agent who controlled the schedules—and profits—of many Black baseball teams on the East Coast.

business affairs, Strong's unique position in New York's baseball circles helped him secure an appointment as president of the Intercity Association, an organization of around one hundred white amateur and semipro teams from New Jersey and New York. Once Strong took over, the association began booking all member teams' games . . . and collecting 10 percent of all gate receipts as a fee for doing so.

Strong wielded tremendous influence—enough to financially make or break a team. This was especially the case for Black teams, which lacked the collective bargaining power that a formal league would provide. Without access to the ballparks, there could be no games. Without games, there could be no revenue. And without revenue, owners couldn't pay their players very much. Eventually, they couldn't operate at all.

Even before taking the helm of the Intercity Association, Strong had staked his claim on Black baseball's profits by cofounding the National Association of Colored Baseball Clubs of the United States and Cuba (NACBC). A *Philadelphia Inquirer* article from October 29, 1906, explained the supposed premise of the new organization:

> The idea is to place colored base ball on a solid business basis and to protect both players and managers from unscrupulous and unreliable managers of independent clubs who engage the colored clubs and unceremoniously cancel the dates at the last moment if so inclined. It is intended to "cut out" all such clubs which treat any of the national agreement clubs in that manner.

The *Inquirer* article also noted that the NACBC sought to protect "the property rights of those engaged in colored base ball as a business, without sacrificing the spirit of competition in the conduct of the game." But with each of the NACBC's five inaugural ball clubs (the Philadelphia Giants, Cuban X-Giants of New York, Cuban Giants of New York, Brooklyn Royal Giants, and Cuban Stars of Havana) having a white owner and/or booking agent at the helm, it was pretty clear which "engaged" parties were of highest priority.

Despite the proclaimed intent, the NACBC proved to be little more than an organized booking network that funneled cash directly into the pockets of Strong, who was the secretary and business manager of the association.

At the same time, Strong's hand hovered over nearly every park in town, and he threatened to refuse entry to any team that tried to go around his reach to schedule its own games. Black teams may have resented Strong's power and the fact that he charged Black teams higher booking fees, but they had no choice in dealing with him—not if they wanted to play games in the lucrative New York market.

In 1908, with the East Coast ball clubs firmly in Strong's pockets, the NACBC decided to schedule some Chicago games for its teams. It was an attempt to wade directly into Rube Foster's territory. But before the eastern teams were scheduled to arrive, the burly pitcher wrote a letter of rebuff to Strong and the other members of the NACBC. In the letter, which was read during the organization's annual meeting, Foster refused to allow his Leland Giants to play any of Strong's clubs, likely as a protest against the booking agent's audacious attempt to maximize profits in a market that he didn't control.

Ultimately, Foster held him off, but Strong's advances made clear what Foster had long known: If Black baseball teams were ever going to reach the level of success and profitability of white teams, Black players, coaches, and team owners would have to protect their own interests.

They would have to organize.

A LEAGUE OF
THEIR OWN

Though Rube Foster would be the first to successfully organize a Black-owned and Black-operated baseball league, he wasn't the first to try.

Black Chicago attorney Beauregard Moseley had become a financial backer of Foster's team, the Chicago Union Giants, in 1905, so he fully understood the money that could be made in baseball. In 1907, Moseley and his partners—a local Black businessman named Robert Jackson and Frank Leland, the team's then-manager—decided to expand their sporting empire. Moseley and company launched the Leland Giants Baseball Club and Amusement Association and changed the Chicago Union Giants' name to the

Leland Giants in the process. Moseley planned to capitalize on the success of the Giants while also operating a skating rink, restaurant, and other attractions. Baseball, however, was always the primary moneymaker of the club, and the Giants were among the best on the Black circuit.

Unfortunately, internal problems soon arose. At the root of the dispute? Leland feared he was losing control of his team to Foster, his ace pitcher and the team's player-manager.

Like most owners, Leland had always paid players out of gate receipts, meaning that if a game was canceled or attendance was very low, players may not have been paid at all. As a result, Leland saw Foster's continued efforts to guarantee player salaries as an attempt to usurp his authority. And while he had initially agreed— along with Jackson and Moseley—to let Foster take over team bookings and player signings, he soon began to regret that decision.

Eventually, Leland left to launch a new team, the Chicago Giants, while Foster, Moseley, and Jackson remained with the Leland Giants. In early 1910, a court ruled that Moseley could continue to use the name "Leland"—even though the team's namesake was gone—and Foster's relationship with the players meant that the core of the original team stayed in place. Then, with the understanding that Black people would have no true place in base-ball if they didn't create one for themselves, Moseley decided to launch the National Negro Baseball League.

With his legal background, Moseley paid careful attention to every detail of the league. Potential franchises were to pay the league a onetime fee of $300 for operational costs. The league would then hire its own umpires, half of whom were to be Black. Regarding revenue splits, winning teams would receive 50 percent of the gate; the losing team would collect 30 percent; and the remaining profits would go to the owner of the stadium in which the game had been played. Appointed league officers, namely a president and treasurer, would be hired to execute those plans.

Moseley had developed a solid blueprint, and teams from New Orleans, Kansas City, and elsewhere expressed interest in joining the burgeoning league. Sadly, the financial realities of Black teams kept the National Negro Baseball League from ever getting off the ground. Playing in a structured circuit like the one Moseley proposed certainly had advantages, but the expenses that arose from league fees, as well as travel to play games against other teams in the new circuit, could devastate a club that wasn't already standing on sure footing. With its winning history and the formidable Foster leading the way, the Leland Giants could afford to join the league. Other teams, however, could not.

* * *

After the 1910 season, Foster made a move that would define the rest of his career as well as the future of Black baseball. After luring away the best Leland Giants players, Foster formed his own team and named it the Chicago American Giants. He also formed a partnership with John M. Schorling, a white tavern owner who had a close relationship with Chicago White Sox owner Charles Comiskey. With this partnership, Foster secured a home field for his team: the White Sox's old stadium, recently abandoned for the new Comiskey Park.

Foster would later call on these connections in white baseball as he began executing his long-term vision to ensure a place for Black athletes in America's new pastime. In the interim, his team was consistently deemed one of the best—if not *the* best—in Black baseball. Because there was no organized league, or set schedule among a group of Black teams, there was no playoff structure to accurately determine which club had finished on top at the end of each season. But Foster's team often made light work of the competition—Black and white—and didn't hesitate to crown itself king.

As the owner and manager of the Chicago American Giants, Rube Foster learned the ins and outs of running a successful baseball team and, eventually, an entire league.

As the Chicago American Giants racked up win after win on the Black baseball circuit, Foster was learning all aspects of running a baseball team. The American Giants' dominance, meanwhile, validated the former pitcher's turn as a manager and co-owner, and that knowledge and respect would prove invaluable when Foster decided to try his own hand at launching a structured Black baseball league.

Foster went public about the need for Black athletes to form their own league as early as 1910, when he wrote an essay called "Success of the Negro as a Ball Player" for the *Indianapolis Freeman* newspaper:

> In my opinion, the time is now at hand when the formation of colored leagues should receive much consideration. In fact, I believe it is absolutely necessary. We have now been in the game for a score of years, and we are no closer related to our white neighbor than when we first started; in fact, we are farther apart as he is going ahead, forming leagues in every little hamlet; and the forming of leagues produces a barrier which we cannot surmount, try as we will, unless we come to understand the heading of.

Foster had seen enough of Moseley's doomed Black baseball league to know that his own success wasn't a foregone conclusion. For starters, Foster would have to persuade other teams to join him, and for that, he took to the pages of the *Chicago Defender.* From November 1919 through January 1920, Foster wrote a series of columns under the banner THE PITFALLS OF BASEBALL, and in those writings, no one—neither player, nor owner—was safe from criticism. If Foster was going to put Black athletes in baseball on a level playing field with whites, it was going to require hard work and sacrifice. It was also going to require owners, players, and even fans to prioritize league interests over personal ones.

In his columns, Foster rebuked players who complained that they weren't being paid well enough by reminding them that their wages were higher than those of most Black men in other occupations. He also chided them for always jumping from team to team in constant search of a larger paycheck—the continual need to attract players, and to later replace them, was making it more difficult for teams to sustain themselves, Foster noted. Finally, Foster demanded that the owners run their teams more professionally, and he chastised those who fought mercilessly with one another without considering the broader effect of their bickering.

Taken together, Foster's impassioned essays were a plea: Black baseball could not continue without organization, and, as he'd stated, the time to organize was now.

✳ ✳ ✳

On February 13, 1920, a group of men in their finest suits walked into the Paseo YMCA in Kansas City, Missouri, in what is now the city's historic 18th and Vine Jazz District, and made history. When they arrived, the representatives from six midwestern teams—plus an attorney and a handful of sportswriters—believed they would be drafting a schedule and working agreement for a new league

Colored Y. M. C. A., 18th and Paseo, Kansas City, Mo.

On February 13, 1920, Rube Foster made history by meeting with owners from other Black, midwestern baseball teams at the Paseo YMCA in Kansas City, Missouri. There he formed the first Negro National League.

proposed by Foster. But the Chicago boss shocked them all by announcing that he had already registered the Negro National League as an official corporation.

Incorporating with the US government was a major step for Foster, one that proved his unwavering commitment to the newly birthed league. He also demonstrated his loyalties by paying, out of his own pocket, the $500 deposit for several team owners who didn't have the money.

"Gentlemen," Foster told the group, "the assets of the baseball club which I represent is more than all the Negro baseball clubs in existence. Still, if it pleases you all, I am willing to throw all these assets upon the mercy of the decision of this body of newspaper men who are present."

Foster wanted to prove that a unified Black league could function as efficiently and effectively as a white one. To that end, his rules were explicit: Players who jumped their contracts and switched teams would be suspended, and any player misconduct or protest of an umpire's on-the-field decision would bring swift disciplinary action.

Black baseball needed a man like Foster—a man who had the on- and off-the-field experience, who could see the challenges of the past as well as the opportunities of the future. Years later, Effa Manley would look back with admiration on Foster's efforts to establish the first successful Negro League, and she would ultimately demand the same excellence from owners and athletes that he did.

Foster's expectations were high and his guidelines strict, but for a while, beginning with the Negro National League's inaugural season in 1920, Black baseball was all the better for it.

NEGRO IMPROVEMENT

It was difficult to pinpoint exactly how many people filled Madison Square Garden on the evening of August 2, 1920, just six months after Rube Foster gathered the best midwestern Black teams beneath the umbrella of the Negro National League. The *Washington Times* reported that twelve thousand were in attendance, while the *New-York Tribune* put the number at fifteen thousand, and the *Baltimore Sun* estimated twenty thousand. But in the end, the exact number didn't matter. Every paper that covered the event—from Ontario, Canada, to Austin, Texas—agreed on the most important thing: The sea of Black faces was shining with joy, the room thunderous with applause.

Surprisingly, it was not a boxing match or an orchestral performance that had drawn tens of thousands to this storied venue in New York City. Instead, the pulsating crowd was there to hear from Marcus Garvey, the Jamaican-born activist who had founded the Universal Negro Improvement Association (UNIA) with the goal of empowering the Black community through complete independence.

Garvey, regal in a luxurious robe of purple, gold, and green, took in the crowd that had pledged their allegiance to him and his Back to Africa movement. "We declare that what is good for the white man in this age is also good for the Negro," Garvey shouted. And, again, the crowd roared.

That Garvey's UNIA had managed to amass such a strong following by 1920 is a remarkable feat, especially considering how recently Garvey had adopted a Black nationalist perspective. When he arrived in the States in 1916, just four years prior, Garvey was a student of Booker T. Washington, the founder of the Tuskegee Institute and one of the Black community's most vocal leaders until his death in 1915. Initially, Garvey respected Washington's attempts to soothe the simmering tensions between white and Black people. But during his early years in America, Garvey had come to question Washington's approach.

Washington was a master at straddling the color line, and he sought to close the gap between white and Black with as little friction as possible. He begged white people to be sympathetic and patient with the Black community that was still struggling to find liberty and stability on the other side of enslavement. Meanwhile, he appeased white fears by asserting that there would be no uprising, that Black people would remain as loyal as they always had and take a moderate approach in their fight for civil rights. Washington believed that if Black people could first improve their own position and become self-reliant—pull themselves up by their bootstraps, so to speak— whites would eventually, hopefully, come to see them as equals.

Though Washington was initially well received throughout the Black community, other Black leaders, including Garvey, ultimately decided more drastic steps needed to be taken if Black people were to ever gain equal footing in American society. Garvey never strayed from his agreement with Washington on the value of Black self-sufficiency, but he abandoned the idea that white people would soon see the error in their racist ways and come around on their own. Like Fleet Walker's, his experiences had provided a harsh reality check, one that couldn't be absolved with good behavior and wishful thinking.

In 1916, the same year that Garvey arrived in Harlem to launch his first branch of the UNIA, Effa Brooks came, too. She was fresh out of high school, a young girl headed to the big city to follow her dreams, and Harlem, a neighborhood in the northern part of Manhattan, was a perfect place in which to settle.

Harlem began as many other communities do—with real estate developers who predict future growth by building housing for people they hope will soon move there. In the beginning, mostly Jewish and Italian immigrants called the neighborhood home, but over time, sales to these communities began to slow. With additional rail and subway lines now crisscrossing much of Manhattan, people had their choice of neighborhood, and Harlem, with its reputation for housing immigrants and the otherwise outcast members of society, fell out of favor.

As developers lamented their empty properties, Philip A. Payton, a Black entrepreneur, saw nothing but opportunity. He persuaded the white property owners to let him manage rentals—and to allow him to rent to Black people. In 1904, Payton launched his Afro-American Realty Company and found ample customers in the thousands of Black renters escaping the savagery of the South.

"Colored Tenants, Attention!" read one of Payton's ads in the *New York Age*. "After much effort I am now able to offer to my people for rent" several apartment houses "of a class never before rented to our people."

By 1914, it was estimated that three-quarters of all Black New York City residents lived in Harlem, including "all blacks of prominence." Thanks to Payton, who was dubbed "the father of Harlem," the bustling neighborhood had become an accessible refuge for Black people of all ilk, from the wide-eyed, ambitious Effa to the bombastic Garvey.

When Effa arrived in Harlem in 1916, the city was an oasis for Black Americans migrating from across the United States and the Caribbean, all of whom were in search of a better life.

And Garvey wasn't the only Black Harlemite with a vision for Negro improvement. Like Garvey, the writer, scholar, and civil rights activist W. E. B. Du Bois also disagreed with Booker T. Washington's theory that Black Southerners could earn educational and economic opportunities, as well as respect, by postponing the fight for full civil rights. But that is where their similarities ended.

While Garvey preached an everyman gospel that sought to empower the Black community as a collective force, Du Bois believed that Black success would be delivered by a select few. As outlined in his 1903 essay, "The Talented Tenth," Du Bois concluded that only one in ten Black men—the elite, the well educated, and, often, the lighter-skinned—could rise as leaders of the entire race. The fair-complexioned Du Bois, who was the first Black person to earn a PhD from Harvard University and the cofounder of the National Association for the Advancement of Colored People (NAACP), was the archetype of his own ideals.

***

Because Harlem developed as a refuge for Black people fleeing from the southern United States, the Caribbean, and other parts of the

Though they had different political views and strategies, W. E. B. Du Bois (*left*) and Marcus Garvey (*right*) shared the same goal: empowerment and equality for Black Americans.

world, it's not surprising that it also played host to multiple Black leaders who differed greatly in their perspectives and politics. Effa was living in Harlem during this blossoming of Black thought leadership, so she was undoubtedly exposed to these contrasting views, to each man's individual efforts to push the Black community forward. And while she never became a strict follower of Garvey, Du Bois, or any other activist, she likely borrowed bits and pieces from each of them.

Like Du Bois, she used her light complexion to her advantage and successfully landed a job as a hatmaker in the all-white world of millinery, no doubt earning much more money than her peers with darker skin.

But like Garvey, she rejected the notion that her fair hue, or anyone else's, should cause discord within the Black community. Effa saw beauty in Black unity, and in due time, she would become a leader in her own right, adding her unique voice to the call for Black civil rights.

NEW NEGROES

As the nation pushed into the third decade of the new century, a reckoning was at hand. First, there were the Red Summer riots of 1919, marked by the deaths of hundreds of Black people at the hands of angry, racist, gun-wielding whites. Then, two years later, the carnage that swept through Chicago and at least a dozen other cities was followed by the 1921 Greenwood, Oklahoma, massacre. Over two days—May 31 and June 1—hundreds more Black lives were cut short, their homes and business looted and torched by whites seeking to destroy a prosperous neighborhood known as Black Wall Street.

Across the country, Black Americans were reeling. But they were also brave. Emboldened.

In Harlem, Black artists were creating seminal works that would define a generation and begin to reposition Black identities within the white psyche as more than ignorant laborers. Poems like Gwendolyn Bennett's "The Heritage" and Langston Hughes's "The Negro Speaks of Rivers" reflected the confluence of Black pride and Black pain, the joy that often arose from unspeakable tragedy. At the same time, Duke Ellington and his dynamic jazz band thrilled audiences at hot spots like the Exclusive Club, while Alain Locke, a writer and philosopher who had become the first Black Rhodes Scholar, served as unofficial principal of the burgeoning Harlem Renaissance.

In an essay titled "Enter the New Negro," from the March 1925 issue of *Survey Graphic* magazine, Locke spoke to the emergence of the modern Black mindset and its refusal to be subservient to any master:

So for generations in the mind of America, the Negro has been more of a formula than a human being—a something to be argued about, condemned or defended, to be "kept down," or "in his place," or "helped up," to be worried with or worried over, harassed or patronized, a social bogey or a social burden . . . By shedding the old chrysalis of the Negro problem we are achieving something like a spiritual emancipation . . . With this renewed self-respect and self-dependence, the life of the Negro community is bound to enter a new dynamic phase, the buoyancy from within compensating for whatever pressure there may be of conditions from without.

As a young woman coming into her own, Effa absorbed the creative, independent spirit of Harlem. She continued to work as a milliner, but she also moonlighted as a model, taking part in fashion shows arranged by Harlem socialites. Effa had learned to sew from her mother, and at one point she made all her garments, including her overcoats, by hand. Modeling gave her the chance to display her innate sense of style while also making key connections with other Harlem women.

Effa also married for the first time after meeting a Black man named Charles Bush in Atlantic City. "I went after him, and I got him," she would later say. Unfortunately, though Effa was successful

After arriving in Harlem, Effa leveraged her love of fashion—and her fair skin—to secure jobs as a hatmaker and model.

in snagging Bush, the marriage only lasted a few months. Her love of baseball, on the other hand, was far more enduring.

The Yankees were Effa's favorite team, and from her apartment, she could walk to the Polo Grounds, the club's home base until 1923. "I was crazy about Babe Ruth," Effa said. "I used to go see all the Yankee games hoping he'd hit the ball out of the park."

The Great Bambino, as Ruth was known, led the Yankees to three World Series championships in the 1920s and was a twelve-time home run leader over the course of his career. Ruth was a pure power hitter who could command a game and a hefty salary; he was both idol and icon, to be sure. He wasn't, however, the only star in baseball.

✳✳✳

In the Midwest, Rube Foster's Negro National League (NNL) was also coming into its own, and Foster's efforts to organize the circuit were reaping considerable rewards. By 1923, the NNL averaged more than sixteen hundred fans at league games—a significant improvement over the paltry crowds that typically attended barnstorming or other independent games. As a whole, the league generated $200,000 in revenue from gate receipts, and because Foster took a 5 percent cut of profits for setting the league schedule and booking games, he netted an average annual salary of $10,000, the equivalent of nearly $150,000 today.

Foster's take was less than what many white booking agents, including Nat Strong, were charging. It was also far less than what some white players—including Babe Ruth, who made $52,000 in 1923—were earning. Nonetheless, Foster was still paid much more than the other NNL owners, a fact that created tension within the league.

After all league expenses (player salaries, umpire fees, equipment, etc.) were deducted from the total gate, the seven other owners each averaged a profit of less than $5,000, or half of what Foster pocketed. Those owners resented the income disparity and believed that Foster's primary focus was the profitability of his Chicago American Giants, not the Negro National League as a whole. But in an essay published in the *Chicago Defender* on December 10, 1921, Foster denied their claims:

> **For 5 per cent I must schedule all games and worry with details. These inexperienced men know nothing of business nor baseball. I have been so engaged day and night in trying to keep other clubs going that I have not been able to see the American Giants practice all season. All of my time has been taken up trying to do things for the other clubs.**

Foster may have publicly defended himself, but he also tried to appease the angry owners, as his vision for success in unity remained strong. He released some of his key players to join the rosters of other teams in a spirit of competitive parity; he reduced his team's financial take for away games, even though the American Giants were often the bigger draw; and he established a league fund to assist teams that ran into financial trouble.

Even without these changes, though, the other owners knew they were better off inside Foster's league than outside it. Indeed, despite Foster's attempt to resign from his league duties in December 1924—a response to an accusation of unfairness from the Detroit Stars' business manager—he was reelected president by a unanimous vote at the next league meeting.

The formation of the NNL had been a boon for Black baseball, serving as proof that Black men could do more than hit, throw, and field. They could, in fact, run their own teams and leagues, too. Still, not everyone in Black baseball benefited from Foster's leadership and the organization that the Negro National League provided.

Most NNL teams were in larger midwestern cities, and although they arranged occasional barnstorming tours that took them throughout the southern and eastern parts of the country, teams based outside the Midwest had to establish a more consistent baseball presence in their communities on their own. Some teams operated independently. Others with more organization and financing created competing circuits.

With Foster serving as mentor, representatives from eleven southern Black baseball teams met in Atlanta in early March of

1920 to form the Negro Southern League. More significantly, Ed Bolden, the co-owner and president of the Hilldale Club in Darby, Pennsylvania, launched a league on the East Coast to directly rival Foster's three years later.

✳✳✳

In 1921 and 1922, Bolden's Hilldale Daisies had been an associate member of Foster's league, but the arrangement became impossible as the regular travel west to play the more centralized NNL teams proved too expensive. Like other NNL owners, Bolden also objected to Foster's total control, so he joined with owners

In 1923, Ed Bolden (*far right*) formed the Eastern Colored League as a direct rival to Rube Foster's Negro National League. He also ran the powerhouse Hilldale Daisies ball club out of Darby, Pennsylvania.

from five other eastern teams to launch the Eastern Colored League (ECL).

The ECL's inaugural season was planned for 1923, but the battle between Rube Foster and Ed Bolden over the new league started well before the first pitch was ever thrown. That four of the six owners of the ECL were white was already bad enough, but Bolden's inclusion of Nat Strong's Brooklyn Royal Giants was more than Foster could handle. The NNL president worried that bringing Strong into the new league would give the cutthroat booking agent even more access to the world of organized Black baseball.

In response, Bolden reminded Foster that it would be nearly impossible to run an East Coast league without Strong's stadium connections; he also pointed out that many of the NNL owners—including Foster, himself—were in business with white men.

Bolden's point could not be ignored: Foster had partnered with John Schorling to form the Chicago American Giants, after all. And it was largely because of Schorling's capital, as well as the stadium access he provided, that the American Giants had become a perennial powerhouse.

As much as Foster and Bolden wished otherwise, the realities of systemic racism made it extremely difficult to run a successful baseball business without the involvement of white people. In the northeast, Bolden was an anomaly: a Black man who owned his own stadium and was able to rebuff Strong's demands to take over his team's bookings . . . at least initially. But what about the other teams in the region, teams run by Black men with equally noble intentions who simply didn't have the resources to stand alone?

In the end, Foster and Bolden arrived at a truce of sorts, and just in time to arrange a first-of-its-kind Colored World Series between the NNL champion Kansas City Monarchs and ECL champion Hilldale Daisies in 1924. The Monarchs won five games to four in a series that further legitimized Black baseball while also generating more than $52,000.

By more closely mirroring the two-league structure of organized white baseball, the NNL and ECL were proving that they were separate but equal. Moreover, by supporting teams in regions across the country, the two leagues were also cultivating a new fan base that many hoped could support Black baseball well into the future. But no one could have predicted the tragedy that lay ahead.

REVERSAL OF FORTUNE

Around six o'clock in the morning on Tuesday, May 26, 1925, Rube Foster awoke to take a bath. He was in Indianapolis, Indiana, a little less than two hundred miles southeast of his hometown of Chicago, and staying at the Eubanks Boarding House in advance of an upcoming baseball game. Four hours later, when Foster still hadn't shown up at the ballpark for the team's scheduled activities, a group of Chicago American Giants, led by captain Bingo DeMoss, decided to check on him.

In Foster's private room, the players found his clothes for the day arranged neatly on the bed. It was strange, given both the late hour and the fact that Foster, himself, was nowhere to be found. But as the men headed toward the shared bathroom down the hall, the puzzle began to assemble itself. The heady stench of gas was drifting into the hallway.

DeMoss pushed through the bathroom door and found Foster unconscious, overtaken by the fumes radiating from a leaky pipe. His arm was splayed across the still-lit water heater, his dark-brown skin singed.

As an ambulance later rushed Foster to the hospital, DeMoss called Foster's wife, Sarah. "If you want to see your husband alive," he said, "come at once."

✳✳✳

Although Foster survived the harrowing ordeal, the formidable pitcher turned NNL president would never be the same. His health continued to suffer, and his behavior became increasingly erratic. In his memoir, infielder George Sweatt recalled the strange antics that he saw from Foster after joining the Chicago American Giants in 1926:

> *Two or three times when I was returning to our apart-ment, I would catch up with Rube and we would walk home together. I noticed that he would be walking alright,*

when all of a sudden he would start to run and I would
have to catch him.

Foster's gas poisoning was a heartbreaking episode in an already successful career that was showing no signs of slowing. But it was also just one part of what broke the man whom many had deemed unbreakable.

Even after his near-death experience, Foster still fought for his people, still hoped that organized white baseball would see the work he'd put into the Negro National League and reconsider its segregated stance. With baseball connections that crossed color lines, Foster wanted to leverage his relationships with Ban Johnson, president of the American League, and John McGraw, manager of the National League's New York Giants, to arrange games between his American Giants and any Major League teams that would have an extra day off while in Chicago to play the White Sox or Cubs.

This practice of exhibition games was fairly commonplace. Before today's era of multimillion-dollar salaries and product endorsements, even top white players played non-league games, not just to make ends meet but also to capitalize on their growing notoriety. For Foster, having his first-rate Chicago American

Giants face off against top white teams wouldn't just fill his team's coffers; it would also prove to white organized baseball that Negro Leagues Baseball was of equal caliber.

Foster met with Johnson and McGraw on February 11, 1926, and while there is no record of exactly what transpired that day, it is believed that Kenesaw Mountain Landis, the commissioner of Major League Baseball, ultimately nixed the idea of his teams regularly engaging in integrated contests.

The decision was a crushing blow for Foster, who had hoisted Black baseball upon his sturdy shoulders and promised victory. In the aftermath, he struggled to bear the truth that, despite his valiant efforts and continued sacrifice, Black baseball was still considered a subpar, second-class knockoff of white baseball. He'd fought for so long—for respect, for opportunity, for equal pay—that perhaps Landis's judgment, along with his declining health and the criticisms from other NNL owners, lead him to believe that the battle was no longer worth fighting.

By late summer, Foster's world was crumbling; the taut ropes that had been desperately holding everything together were beginning to snap. Sweatt, who was living on the second floor of Foster's apartment building in Chicago, was there the night that it all came crashing down.

We were sitting upstairs and his wife hollered, "Oh no, don't do that!" So I ran down, knocked on the door, and called out, "Mrs. Foster, is there anything wrong?" She said, "There's something wrong with Rube, he's just going crazy down here. I'm going to have to call the law."

Foster was admitted to Chicago's Psychopathic Hospital on September 1, 1926. After eight days of observation and examination—days marked by violent outbursts and memory lapses—Foster was declared mentally unstable and committed to an institution in Kankakee, Illinois.

* * *

Foster's absence was devastating for all in his orbit. In 1928, two years after Foster was committed, John Schorling sold the Chicago American Giants to a white florist named William Trimble. Sarah Foster claimed that her husband, though incapacitated, still had ownership rights to the team, but because there was no written documentation of any such agreement, she received no proceeds from the sale.

The Negro National League, meanwhile, suffered its own troubles. Expenses continued to increase as the growing popularity of the game drove player salaries higher and an effort to stage contests in various locales put a burden on transportation costs. Players were still jumping from one team to the next, and without a centralized figure like Foster to assist with the scheduling and booking of games, clubs struggled to fill their calendar with profitable matches.

Yet even after the Negro National League's glory days had passed, Black teams continued to rally on the baseball diamond. In many cases, they were led by Black men like Abe Manley—men who looked to marry their search for financial sustainability with their love of the game.

✳✳✳

Abe Manley was born in 1885 in Hertford, North Carolina, and bred in the Quaker tradition that emphasized strict rules and a strong work ethic. He spent his formative years helping out on the family farm and tending to his father's horses, but the life of manual labor and daylight-to-sundown work hours never suited him. As often as he could, Abe found time to play baseball, the new sport sweeping the country.

When Abe entered high school with no real job prospects, his father encouraged him to begin working in the local sawmill. Abe obliged, but soon after he started at the mill, he lost his right index finger in a tragic accident. The mishap was painful, but it was also productive, serving as the final push Abe needed to leave his hometown, and the drudgery of rural life, for good. Abe had discovered, like so many others, that options were few for Black men and women in the South, and he eagerly set out in search of the "warmth of other suns."

After moving to Norfolk, to Brooklyn, and then back to Norfolk again, Abe finally settled in Camden, New Jersey. Once there, he fell in love with Ed Bolden's Hilldale Club.

The Daisies were based just across the Delaware River in Darby, Pennsylvania, but team owner Bolden had shrewdly secured a long-term lease on a Camden ballpark, essentially giving Hilldale two home fields. So while Effa cheered on the Babe, Abe rooted for Raleigh "Biz" Mackey, a future Hall of Fame catcher with an equally dangerous bat.

Eventually, after witnessing the Negro Leagues' boom years

of the mid-1920s, Abe decided to throw his hat onto the field by purchasing his own team, the Camden Leafs. Under normal circumstances, he may have seen success with his independent Black club. But Abe bought his team in 1929, and in 1929, things were far from normal.

That year, the country sank into a deep economic depression, draining whatever lifeblood Black baseball had left. In fact, by the time the stock market officially crashed on October 24, 1929, the downturn had already swept through the Black community. Businesses were feeling the pinch long before then, and it was Black workers who saw their anemic wages and hours cut first. No money was left for the frivolities of baseball—not for a husband buying tickets for a family of four, or a team owner trying to purchase uniforms for the season.

Abe's team folded at the end of the 1929 season, just as economic darkness began to blanket the entire country, including the baseball business. To make matters worse, the once prosperous Negro National League was about to receive its most devastating blow yet: Rube Foster passed away on December 9, 1930, at the age of fifty-one; he'd never once left the Kankakee State Hospital after being admitted in 1926.

When Rube Foster died on December 9, 1930, he left behind an incredible baseball legacy, as well as questions about the future of the Negro Leagues.

On December 15, less than a week after Foster's death, three thousand mourners gathered to pay their respects to the greatest man Black baseball had ever known. In addition to being one of the best pitchers of his time, Foster was a friend to all players, the rare executive who knew what it was like to be on both sides of the ball. More than that, though, Foster had made the dream of an organized Black league a reality. He proved that success could, indeed, be found in unity. But as Foster was laid to rest, many, including a writer for the *Chicago Defender*, wondered if Black baseball could be resurrected, or if the future of the Negro Leagues would be buried with him:

We hesitate to predict the future of the infant baseball industry which Mr. Foster nurtured among our people. Already it seems a bit groggy and appears toppling.

FAIR PLAY

Before and after his short stint as the owner of the Camden Leafs, Abe ran the Rest-A-While Club, the premier political and social gathering place for Camden's Black community. The Rest-A-While was a place for prominent men to convene over drinks and cigars, and it was the corporate office for Abe's business ventures, too. Like many Black men of his era, Abe filled his business portfolio with a mix of the legitimate and illicit; even as he legally purchased and managed real estate holdings around the city, he also ran a profitable numbers racket.

Although the US government didn't allow states to run their

own lotteries until the 1960s, Americans had been gambling for decades, placing daily bets on a lucky number (or three) in hopes of hitting a jackpot. Back then, before the states took over, those illegal gambling operations were run by men and women who amassed small fortunes collecting the bets of community members, paying prize money to any winners, and pocketing the surplus cash. To play, participants chose a three-digit number and placed their bets with a policy banker. Later in the day, the winning numbers were pulled from a predetermined, verifiable source—say, the daily balance of the US Treasury, or the total of all bets received at the local horse racetrack.

It's not surprising that numbers operations were especially popular in low-income communities, where unemployment and stagnant wages left people desperate for a windfall. But in Black communities, the illegal numbers game did much more than provide the hope of a quick payday.

Because policy bankers paid out an average of only $600 for every $1,000 in collected bets, those who ran their own racket made a substantial profit. The numbers game was, in fact, one of the few ways that Black men and women could earn a lucrative living in the

1920s and '30s. What's more, those policy bankers often reinvested their profits into their local communities, subsequently becoming revered members of Black society.

When banks refused to lend capital to Black borrowers, policy bankers stepped in. When city and state governments neglected to fund programs and facilities in Black communities, policy bankers stepped in. When Black consumers craved their own restaurants and clubs and retail stores—where they could shop and eat and drink in peace—policy bankers stepped in, starting businesses that shielded their ill-gotten gains while also providing necessary services. And when unemployment left Black men and women destitute and struggling to provide for their families, policy bankers stepped in, hiring them as numbers runners tasked with gathering the day's bets.

In Black neighborhoods, the numbers game represented a justifiable means to a somewhat satisfying end. But for all its virtues, it was still considered criminal—and any criminal activity is sure to attract its share of danger. Indeed, policy bankers often faced competition from competitors who wanted to push them out and take over their businesses; in many cases, these rivalries were neither clean nor fair.

In the fall of 1932, the building that housed Abe's Rest-A-While

Club was bombed, reportedly by rival numbers bankers from Philadelphia. The incident, a sure sign of more peril to come, drove Abe out of Camden and into Harlem, where he began searching for a legitimate business in which to funnel the money he'd made.

In Harlem, he also found a wife.

✳✳✳

Effa became Mrs. Abe Manley on June 15, 1933, and the couple quickly settled into their new apartment in Harlem's Sugar Hill neighborhood. Besides the Manleys, Sugar Hill was home to many wealthy, well-educated Black New Yorkers, including attorney Thurgood Marshall and musicians Duke Ellington and Cab Calloway.

Abe Manley and Effa Brooks married on June 15, 1933, and became the perfect partners—in life and in baseball.

In the years before World War I, it would have been unheard of for the Manleys to navigate the same social circles as men like Marshall and Ellington. Back then, the Black upper class had been reserved for morally upright, well-educated, and lighter-skinned men and women who, as a result of those perceived advantages, often had higher household incomes. But the rules had softened in northern cities after the war. Most notably, a class of "upper shadies," or people who earned their wealth from illicit activities, were allowed entry. This was especially the case for Black people who, like Abe, leveraged the spoils of their improper activities for the benefit of the larger Black community.

Abe's wealth didn't just afford Effa access to the top tier of Black society; it also gave her an opportunity to enjoy life's finer things. When Effa accompanied Abe to pick up her engagement ring from Tiffany, the legendary New York jewelry store, she got a kick out of seeing the white salesclerks stare in shocked silence as Abe, a brown-skinned man approaching fifty, stepped to the counter to pay for a five-carat diamond for his much younger fiancée—a woman who appeared to be white. Later in life, Effa also remembered how Abe liked to keep her dressed in furs and expensive clothes as a way to prove their financial stability and assure their employees that they would be paid on time.

It would have been easy for Effa to simply host parties and attend social events, floating in the bubble of high-class Harlem, but she remained sympathetic to those who weren't as financially fortunate as she and Abe were. After all, the artistic Renaissance of the 1920s had affected just a small portion of Harlem's Black community; for the men and women who worked in low-level service and domestic jobs, it had meant scarcely little. What's more, many intellectuals, artists, and other leaders of the New Negro movement had made a concerted effort to avoid telling the stories of everyday people in their depictions of Black Harlem, choosing, instead, to focus on more privileged Black perspectives. These spit-shined narratives may have been more palatable to the white patrons who helped to fund the Renaissance, but they effectively silenced the voices of the Black working class, who were toiling in anonymity.

In *A Renaissance in Harlem: Lost Voices of an American Community*, edited by Lionel Bascom, Bascom explains this further, likening the Renaissance's intentional focus on well-to-do Black people to a sort of secret code:

> *This code would safeguard the pristine image of uptown life created by those writers who were embraced by the white New York publishing houses; the books and stories they wrote would ultimately become the canon of*

all modern black literature and of a renaissance that oc-
curred in Harlem. As celebrated as this writing was, it
did not present a comprehensive portrait of Harlem or its
people.

To say that the Harlem Renaissance didn't paint a comprehen-sive portrait is a vast understatement. When Abe and Effa settled in Sugar Hill, it was a long thirteen years after Marcus Garvey had enraptured the crowd at Madison Square Garden with promises of Black prosperity and independence. By 1933, Garvey had been deported to his homeland of Jamaica after a stunning fall from grace, the cumulative result of a series of disparaging remarks made against other Black leaders, a well-publicized meeting with the KKK, a criminal conviction for mail fraud, and an anti-Semitic rant in the aftermath of that conviction.

Meanwhile, W. E. B. Du Bois was charting a new course, in both his career and political views. Frustrated by the slow rate of racial progress being made by the NAACP, the activist resigned as the editor of the NAACP's magazine, *The Crisis*, and left Sugar Hill, where he'd also been living, to take a teaching position in Atlanta in 1933.

Most notably, after witnessing how President Franklin Delano Roosevelt's New Deal efforts to revive the American economy had favored whites—how even the well-bred, well-educated Black men of "Talented Tenth" stature failed to fully overcome systemic racism—Du Bois began advocating for solidarity and self-sufficiency among *all* Black people. If Roosevelt and other powerful white men refused to welcome them into white society, he reasoned, Black Americans should simply create a society of their own. "It must be remembered," Du Bois wrote in January 1934, "that in the last quarter of a century, the advance of the colored people has been mainly in the lines where they themselves[,] working by and for themselves, have accomplished the greatest advance."

This was the Harlem in which Abe and Effa found themselves in the early 1930s. After a period of hope and promise, the average Black Harlem resident, someone who had been overlooked by the Renaissance's glamorous facade, was struggling to survive. For these maids and street sweepers, grandiose dreams of political and social advancements came secondary to the daily needs of taking care of their families, of buying food and paying rent. Effa, though privileged in her own right, saw these struggles and decided that she wasn't just going to sit around and be Abe Manley's pampered wife.

She was going to get involved.

✳ ✳ ✳

At a dinner in early 1934, Effa had a conversation with William Davis, editor of the Black weekly newspaper the *New York Amsterdam News,* about how difficult it was for Black women to find decent jobs in Harlem. She explained that many of them served as domestics, barely making ends meet as they cleaned the homes of white women, cooked for them, and cared for their children.

In the 1930s, 125th Street was the hub of Harlem life. But while many of the retailers were happy to welcome Black customers, they were less inclined to hire them as employees.

Davis agreed with Effa's sentiment and drew her attention to the L. M. Blumstein department store on 125th Street. Of all the stores lining the Harlem corridor, Blumstein's was the largest. It was also a favorite destination for Black shoppers who lived in the area.

"Mrs. Blumstein's a fine woman," said Davis about Mrs. L. M. Blumstein, who co-owned the department store with her brother-in-law William Blumstein. "I believe, if you asked her, she'd hire a Negro."

Blumstein's department store had hired some Black employees, but it had hired only a few, and only in low-level positions like elevator operators and janitors. Effa's goal was to get Black women hired as salesclerks, a more visible and better-paid position. She knew that persuading the Blumsteins to buck racial norms and change their hiring practices would be difficult, but, with Davis's advice, she accepted the challenge and quickly enlisted the help of others. Effa formed the Harlem Women's Association with other socially conscious Black women of Harlem's upper class, and in February 1934, they held their first meeting in the Manleys' apartment.

The organization's efforts were slow going at first, with

the women disagreeing on the most effective way to persuade Mrs. Blumstein to hire more Black employees. Finally, after some deliberation, one of the members mentioned that her minister might be interested in getting involved, that maybe he could help them achieve the results they desired more quickly. Much to their delight, the Reverend John H. Johnson, rector of St. Martin's Episcopal Church, *was* happy to assist.

In cities across the country, Black leaders were merging Du Bois's new theory on Black self-help with the economic realities of the time. The premise for these civil rights crusades was simple: Amid the push for an integrated workforce, Black customers should only spend their money at establishments that hired Black employees. Johnson was a staunch supporter of what became known as the "Don't Buy Where You Can't Work" campaign, and he suggested that Effa's association stage a similar approach with Blumstein's.

***

After changing its name from the Harlem Women's Association to the Citizens League for Fair Play, Effa's group launched its charge against Blumstein's department store on April 8, 1934. That Sunday, Johnson stood before his congregants and asked them to gather their Blumstein's sales receipts over a two-week period. The goal was to show just how valuable Black shoppers were to the store's operations, and the resulting mountain of evidence was glaring: Over fourteen days, Black consumers spent more than $7,000 at the department store, or just over $133,000 in today's dollars.

Surely, Effa and Johnson assumed, this data would be enough to shift the seemingly immovable position of the Blumsteins in their favor. Blumstein's dependence on the Black community was now evident, in black and white, undeniable and unavoidable. The owners would have no choice but to acknowledge this and change their hiring practices accordingly.

Receipts in hand, Johnson met with William Blumstein. Johnson was tenacious but also careful not to push too hard; he knew that offending the Blumsteins could put the entire campaign in jeopardy.

Johnson asked that just one Black woman be trained and hired as a salesclerk. But even as Blumstein admitted that the receipts from Black shoppers accounted for 75 percent of the store's total sales, he refused the reverend's request.

When Johnson returned with the news, it was like a punch in the gut to Effa and the countless Black women relying on the league's success. Still, there was no giving up. Sending letters and politely asking the Blumsteins to hire Black workers may not have worked, but by May, the league was ready with a new strategy: a full-scale boycott and picket line.

For six weeks, Effa and others marched in front of the Blumstein's entrance, while more than three hundred other churches, businesses, and civic organizations lent their support. Harlem's two Black newspapers, meanwhile, were mixed in their backing. Perhaps fearful that white advertisers of the paper would withdraw their funding, William Davis, who'd first suggested that Effa appeal to Mrs. Blumstein, criticized the boycott and refused to publicize it in the *Amsterdam News*. The league did, however, receive support from the *New York Age*, a competing Black paper that actively covered the group's efforts and progress. This publicity—particularly the amplification of the message that Black consumers should avoid shopping at Blumstein's until the store hired Black salesclerks—played a key role in the boycott's eventual success.

Like the Montgomery Bus Boycott that would kick off in Alabama just over two decades later, the Blumstein's protest stopped the flow of cash from Black hands to white pockets. And like any responsible business owners concerned with their bottom line, the Blumsteins were forced to reconsider their stance.

Finally, in mid-July, William Blumstein agreed to meet with Johnson, Effa, attorney Richard Cary, and *New York Age* editor Fred Moore, to find a mutually agreeable resolution.

This was great news for Effa. She had confidence and determination burning hot in her veins—and she wasn't going to come out of that meeting without getting exactly what she, and the rest of Black Harlem, wanted.

A WINNING TEAM

For two hours on Thursday, August 2, 1934, Effa and her allies sat sequestered with William Blumstein in his office. After introductions, Blumstein opened the discussion by describing the many troubles he'd faced as a result of the protest. He was old, he said. Too old for such a public battle like this. And the business was struggling. Ever since the league had called for Black customers to stop shopping at Blumstein's, the store had suffered considerable losses.

Effa and Johnson listened intently to Blumstein's pleas, nodding where appropriate. But if the businessman was hoping for sympathy—or for the Citizens League to lessen its demands in light of his "struggles"—he wasn't going to get it.

"The league has not receded one inch from the position we had taken up when we first approached you," Johnson told Blumstein. "Nor are we prepared to."

There was a lot of back-and-forth then—more emotional appeals from Blumstein and more refusals to concede from Johnson. But the conversation was going nowhere. Finally, Effa decided to add her own voice to the debate.

"You know, Mr. Blumstein, we think just as much of our young colored girls as you do of your young white girls, and there's just no work for them," she said. "The only thing they could find to do is work in someone's home as a maid or become prostitutes."

In an instant, the room fell silent; each man's jaw went slack with shock.

Women played a peripheral role in 1930s society, and they were more likely seen than heard. Effa knew this, but she also knew that she had been invited to this meeting because of her key leadership role during the protest, as well as her representation of the young Harlem women they were fighting for. Effa had something to say, so she took advantage of her opportunity and said it.

"Oh, Mrs. Manley!" Cary cried, his face flush with embarrassment. "Don't say such a thing!"

Effa took in the stunned expressions of the others in the room, but she didn't waver. Her mention of prostitution didn't just catch everyone off guard, it had also brought the issues facing young Black women into clear focus—just as she'd hoped it would.

"Well, it's the truth," she calmly responded as the men continued to stare. "I'm only telling you what's true."

✳✳✳

Two days later, on August 4, the front page of the *New York Age* was crowned with a declaration of triumph: BLUMSTEIN'S TO HIRE NEGRO CLERKS.

Blumstein's department store was the target of a "Don't Buy Where You Can't Work" campaign initiated by Effa and other members of Harlem's Black community.

Beneath the headline, just adjacent to a story detailing the "important Negro history" that the Citizens League had helped to write, was a statement issued by William Blumstein and dated July 26, 1934:

In recognition of the principles asserted by the Rev. Dr. J. H. Johnson as the leader of and spokesman for the colored people of Harlem and in deference to his wishes and the wishes of the people he represents, L. M. Blumstein has decided to increase the personnel of its working staff by employing colored clerical and sales help and will take on fifteen (15) between now and August 15th and twenty (20) more in the month of September, and thereafter such number as in the judgment of the management business conditions will warrant.

Both parties to the controversy hope to maintain the friendly relations hereby established and trust in the good faith of each other to carry out the amicable arrangements we arrived at today.

Though Effa's role in swaying the conversation went unmentioned in William Blumstein's statement, fifteen Black women were immediately hired by Blumstein's department store—enough for the Citizens League to cancel the boycott.

But there was a slight problem. Although many of the picketers had been lower-income, darker-skinned Black women—women who had the most to gain from a victory against Blumstein's—they weren't the ones who benefited from the hiring spree. Of the fifteen hires, most were fair-skinned and middle class. Indeed, it seemed that even after the Blumsteins' reversal, the Black women who didn't fit traditional, almost-white standards of beauty were still more likely to earn money scrubbing floors than standing behind a counter at the cushy department store.

What's more, the league had no way to hold the department store accountable once the signs were packed away and the cameras stopped flashing. After the initial fifteen Black women were hired, the twenty additional hires promised by the Blumsteins never materialized.

The outcome was a harsh reminder that racial progress wasn't perfect or proportionate—a confirmation, perhaps, of what Garvey and Du Bois had already learned, and what others eventually would. As whites began to create more space for Blacks in the 1930s and beyond, that space was limited and tightly controlled. There could be only a handful of Black people at a time, and those chosen must be acceptable in appearance and demeanor. Even today,

Black workers in predominantly white industries may feel pressure to dress, act, and look a certain way. And in highly visible roles—like those on prime-time television shows, for example—lighter skin tends to be an advantage.

Effa would continue to grapple with this reality as her career progressed, but in that moment, in the sticky heat of a Harlem summer, the Citizens League considered the Blumstein's boycott a smashing success. For Effa, who would remain a champion of Black empowerment for the rest of her life, the win was proof that righteous indignation could be necessary and productive.

No reports detail exactly how Abe felt after seeing his wife effectively dismantle institutional racism right before his eyes, but he must have been proud. And with his entrepreneurial spirit always yearning for a new opportunity, it may have been Effa's turn as vocal leader and master negotiator that caused Abe to consider another stint in the baseball business.

While Abe's previous turn as team owner had certainly been sabotaged by the Great Depression, it's also true that he didn't take to the business side of the sport as readily as he did to the on-field operations. Abe was a player's owner, the guy who would hang in the dugout and climb onto the bus for road trips, happily talking stats and strategy. But contract negotiations, publicity, and book-keeping? Those were not his strong suits.

He'd failed miserably in the business of baseball before, but Abe had a feeling his fortunes might be on the upswing. Effa's civic involvement had given her a crash course in reading a room, asserting herself, and effecting change. Even better: She was on Abe's team.

✳ ✳ ✳

On November 13, 1934, the newly relaunched Negro National League (NNL) granted Abe a franchise for the New York–based Brooklyn Eagles.

Abe decided to purchase his second Black baseball team in 1935, and with a smart, outspoken Effa by his side, he knew that his odds for winning were greatly improved.

Representatives of the league were excited to welcome the Eagles, along with the New York Cubans, who would also play their inaugural NNL season in 1935. Before that year, the league didn't have a team presence in New York, despite the more than four hundred thousand Black people who lived in the baseball-loving city, representing a built-in fan base if there ever was one. To capitalize on the seemingly wide-open market, Abe arranged for the Eagles to play home games at Ebbets Field when the Major League Brooklyn Dodgers weren't in town. For other contests, the Eagles would travel the country by bus, picking up games wherever there was dirt and a crowd, just like the other Black teams.

In a move that is similar to modern expansion drafts intended to fill the rosters of clubs that have been newly added to professional sports leagues, the NNL required each of its existing teams to provide one or two players to the Brooklyn Eagles. Abe then sent his new manager, veteran first baseman Ben Taylor, to find the remaining players he needed. With Abe's deep pockets and promises of healthy, prompt salaries, Taylor was able to recruit men from independent teams who didn't have binding contracts. His top get was a young, right-handed pitcher named Leon Day, a hurler with a blazing fastball and a future in the National Baseball Hall of Fame.

In the meantime, Abe went to work convincing his wife of the benefits of owning a baseball team.

While Effa was busy pushing for social change, Abe had continued to follow his beloved Black baseball, and he wasn't happy with what he saw. With Rube Foster long gone and the Black community still buckling under the weight of the Depression, teams struggled to break even, let alone turn a profit. Abe thought the teams were ill-organized, overly dependent on barnstorming games, and ultimately "going nowhere fast."

"There's a lot of talent on those teams," he told Effa, "but it's being wasted."

Effa's love of baseball didn't directly translate into the necessary skills for running a team. But like everything else she did, she was fully committed, eager to support her husband, and hopeful that, just maybe, she could make a name for herself, too.

As it turned out, the Manleys' decision to jump into Black baseball just before the '35 season couldn't have been better timed. Black baseball was going through a transformation then, and it was led by men whose dreams extended far beyond the dusty ball fields of barnstorming tours. They were ambitious and competitive, and they were determined to prove that the Negro Leagues didn't die with Rube Foster.

PART II

Black in Business

KING(S) OF DIAMONDS

As it had once been a fertile breeding ground for Octavius Catto and other pioneers of Black baseball, Pennsylvania became the birthplace of the resurrected Negro National League that drew its first tenuous breaths in 1933. But Rube Foster's successors weren't based in Catto's Philadelphia. Instead, they were three hundred miles west, in Pittsburgh.

✳✳✳

According to official records, Republican Charles H. Kline was mayor of Pittsburgh from 1926 to 1933. That may have been true, but William Augustus "Gus" Greenlee was the city's undisputed king.

Born in Marion, North Carolina, Greenlee arrived in Pittsburgh in 1916, running as much from the slow-moving South as his parents' demands that he graduate from college and start a respectable career. Greenlee's father was a well-paid brick-and-mason contractor who afforded his family financial comfort. His mother, meanwhile, was the product of a wealthy white man's illicit affair with his slave; and like Effa, Greenlee's mother inherited her father's fair skin and passed it down to her children. All of that is to say: Young Gus had as many advantages as a Black man in the early twentieth century could hope for.

Greenlee's siblings made the most of their favor—two brothers became doctors, one a lawyer—but Greenlee had other aspirations. Upon arriving in Pittsburgh, he spent time shining shoes, working in a steel mill, and serving as a chauffeur before saving enough money to buy a taxicab and go into business for himself. After a brief tour in the army during World War I, Greenlee finally began his swift ascent to the top of Pittsburgh's Black social class. And like Abe Manley, he didn't exactly take the legal route.

During the height of Prohibition, when it was illegal to produce or sell any alcoholic beverages in the United States, Greenlee became a rumrunner, using his taxi to transport clandestine beer and whiskey around town. The money was good, but nothing like the cash he stacked after helping to bring the numbers game to Pittsburgh. Though his gambling business was only moderately successful at the outset, Greenlee soon capitalized on a fateful turn of events that would lay the foundation for a massive empire.

For numbers bettors, there were as many ways to choose a number to play as there were people who played the game. Some may have chosen the birthday of a deceased great-uncle, while others picked the number of their first big-city apartment. This variance typically meant that lots of different numbers were played on any given day, but on a sweltering day in August 1930, something strange happened. Hundreds of gamblers hit on the same number, sending many policy bankers into a financial tailspin.

Without enough money to cover all the winning payouts, some bankers paid what they could and closed up shop; many simply left town. But Greenlee dug deep to cover all his clients' winning tickets. He then took over the abandoned territories of his former competitors and saw his profits skyrocket. When the dust settled, Greenlee was collecting up to $25,000 a day in bets and employing five hundred men as runners.

Savvy as he was, Greenlee was always on the lookout for his next investment opportunity. His biggest was an old hotel on the corner of Wylie Avenue and Crawford Street that he turned into an upscale nightclub named the Crawford Grill. It became the go-to spot in Pittsburgh's all-Black Hill District, the place where Greenlee conducted his business and solidified his czarlike reputation.

Greenlee was shrewd, but he was also fair and concerned about his community. The Depression hung heavy on the Hill, and it was Greenlee who lent money to out-of-work men and dropped off bags of groceries to single mothers. He covered rent payments and doctor's bills for Black people who had fallen on hard times, fashioning himself as a protector of the people—and even hiring a part-time publicist to spread the word.

In addition to running the Crawford Grill in Pittsburgh's Hill District, Gus Greenlee owned the Pittsburgh Crawfords baseball team and was determined to make his name in the world of Black baseball.

It was because of Greenlee's reputation for generosity that a ragtag group of semipro baseball players showed up at the Crawford Grill one evening in 1930 to ask him for help. The boys were talented but broke, and without a benefactor, the team would be forced to disband. Greenlee rebuffed their initial request, but a week later he'd changed his mind. He decided to buy the team and pay every player a regular salary, much to the delight of the athletes, who were used to the unpredictability of wages based on ticket sales.

Greenlee had already become the king of the Hill; now he planned to reign over the baseball diamond, too. The only issue? There was already a dominant Black team in town, and its owner wasn't about to cede control to a gangster like Gus.

***

On the surface, Cumberland "Cum" Willis Posey Jr. and Gus Greenlee were polar opposites. The southern-born Greenlee was a hefty man whose weight reflected his love of excess. Posey, meanwhile, was slight in stature and a native of Homestead, less than ten miles outside Pittsburgh. Perhaps most important—to Posey, at least—the Pennsylvania native earned an honest living. He ran neither numbers nor rum, making it a point to avoid the seedy activities that Greenlee seemed drawn to. Yet despite these differences, the two men actually had a lot in common.

Like Greenlee's, Posey's family also had means; in fact, the

A lifelong athlete, Cum Posey moved up the ranks within the Homestead Grays organization, beginning as a player and ultimately becoming owner of one of the best teams in Negro Leagues history.

Poseys were one of the richest Black families in western Pennsylvania. After learning the mechanics of ship engines while working as a deck sweeper on a ferry, Posey's father, Cap, used that knowledge to become a riverboat pilot and engineer. He later began constructing his own barges, ultimately amassing a large fleet. Posey's mother also placed the same value on education that Greenlee's mother did. She was the first Black woman to graduate from Ohio State University and the first to teach there, so she naturally expected her children to follow in her enlightened footsteps. But like Greenlee, who'd dropped out of college after one year, Posey ultimately decided that studying wasn't the best use of his time.

Posey was an athlete at heart, spending far more time on basketball courts and baseball diamonds than in his books. After starring on the Homestead High basketball team, he later played varsity hoops at Penn State, earning a starting spot as a sophomore. Summers were for baseball, though, and Posey joined the all-Black Homestead Grays (initially called the Murdock Grays) in 1911.

For all his life, sports were Posey's passion. He would eventually be recognized for his talents as both athlete and executive, becoming the only person inducted into the National Baseball Hall of Fame as well as the Naismith Memorial Basketball Hall of Fame. But as a young man, Posey's love of sports seemed only to get in the way.

Even as Posey's well-heeled background and light skin earned him entrance into multiple predominantly white universities, his poor grades kicked him back out, forcing him to refocus and try again. This happened repeatedly until, after seeing only limited progress with his studies, he finally gave up on college for good. With that, Posey returned home to Pittsburgh to work for a railway mail service and to, of course, play baseball.

Posey was still playing for the Grays, and with his years of baseball experience, he eventually began taking on greater responsibility with the team. He became the club's captain in 1916, field manager in 1917, and secretary in 1918. Then, in 1920—just as Rube Foster was launching the first Negro National League, but a full ten years before Greenlee even considered jumping into Black baseball—Posey became the co-owner of the Grays when he and a local businessman named Charlie Walker purchased the team outright.

Posey's foray into the business of baseball was the natural next step for someone who'd spent his whole life around the game. Like Foster before him, Posey had a camaraderie with his players because he'd been one, and he had firsthand knowledge of what it took to field a successful team. Greenlee, on the other hand, knew little about the game. Initially, at least, Black baseball was just an alternative path to cash and clout.

By the time Greenlee and his well-paid Crawfords burst onto the city's Black baseball circuit, the Grays had been dominating local competition for decades. At the same time, Posey had established himself as a capable leader with a vision for the future that extended far beyond his own roster. Though he'd never joined Rube Foster's Negro National League or the rival Eastern Colored League, Posey was ready to bring a formal structure back to Black baseball in the early 1930s. But to do that, he would have to go through Greenlee and the Crawfords.

Greenlee may have been the inexperienced rookie next to the veteran Posey, but he was fully determined to prove that the Crawfords—not the Grays—were the premier Black team in Pittsburgh.

BORN AGAIN

During the 1931 season, Gus Greenlee made his boldest move toward overtaking Posey as Pittsburgh's titan of Black baseball: acquiring a long, lean, right-handed pitcher named Satchel Paige. Paige was known for his blazing fastball and massive strikeout totals, and Greenlee was hopeful that Paige's arm could carry his Crawfords all the way to the top.

Given the name Leroy when he was born in Mobile, Alabama, Paige earned his moniker while carrying the bags of white travelers who passed through the local train station. For each piece of luggage he dropped off at a nearby hotel, Paige earned about ten cents. It wasn't bad money for an elementary school–aged boy with no real skills, but it wasn't good enough for Paige. He'd been helping to bring in money for his family of fourteen since he was six years old, and he was always looking to make more. So with a pole and some rope, Paige created a device that allowed him to carry three or four bags at once. When a friend saw Paige carrying the contraption, he told him he looked like a "walking satchel tree," and the nickname stuck.

When Paige wasn't trying to earn money, he was playing baseball, though he lacked the fundamentals that would eventually position him as one of the best pitchers in the sport. Paige could always throw fast and hard, but it wasn't until he was sentenced to reform school as a precocious twelve-year-old that he honed his technique. "I traded five years of freedom to learn how to pitch…," he later said. "They were not wasted years at all. It made a real man out of me."

Paige pitched his first professional game in 1926 as a member of the Chattanooga White Sox. He later bounced around and played for teams in Birmingham, Baltimore, and Cleveland. By the time he was approached by Greenlee, Paige had become one of Black baseball's biggest draws, a man who was feared by batters and adored by fans. Paige also knew his worth—that he could change a team's fortune, and his own, with his nasty arsenal of pitches—so he switched teams unrepentantly, always following the owner with the biggest checkbook. Temporarily, that distinction belonged to Greenlee.

Paige's biggest game of the '31 season was against the rival Grays in early August. Greenlee had likely been yearning for the moment when he could trot out his new star and watch Posey's face harden with envy. Paige, for his part, didn't disappoint.

Pitcher Harry Kincannon started the game for Greenlee's club and managed to hold off the Grays at the beginning of the contest. After three innings, the Crawfords were on top with a score of 7–2, but things quickly went downhill in the fourth. When the Grays added five to their tally, evening the score at 7–all, Paige was brought in to relieve the floundering Kincannon.

Paige was brilliant, striking out six Grays players through the rest of the game and holding Posey's team scoreless. To aid his efforts, the Crawford bats added three more runs, pulling away to a 10–7 victory. Greenlee was so thrilled with Paige's performance that he later offered to pay the ace a salary of $700 for the month, a significant increase over the $250 they'd agreed to.

Needless to say, not everyone in Pittsburgh was happy about Paige's dominance. So while Greenlee continued building what he believed would be the best team in Black baseball, Posey set his own plans in motion. He decided to build an entire league.

✳✳✳

In 1932, Posey launched his new East-West League, but instead of extending an unrestricted invitation to his crosstown rivals, the Grays' boss decided that the Crawfords could join his organization only if they met several outlandish requirements:

First, Posey demanded full control of the Crawfords' schedule and roster for the next five years, presumably to limit competition between Greenlee's team and his own. Posey wanted the authority to veto any games played in the Grays' territory, as well as the right to transfer some Crawfords players to other teams.

Posey also wanted to establish a salary cap that would limit how much Greenlee could spend to acquire players. Even in today's professional sports leagues, salary caps exist to level the playing field by preventing big-market teams with more money—like, say, the New York Yankees—from using their wealth to outspend small-market teams—like the Kansas City Royals—and sign all the best talent. With the newly acquired Paige racking up wins, Posey knew that Greenlee would spare no expense in assembling the best Black players around him, and Posey was determined to thwart his efforts.

Finally, if the Crawfords were to become a member of the East-West League, Posey required that his brother, Seward Posey, be hired as the club's manager, most likely to keep an extremely close eye on Greenlee's business affairs.

Not surprisingly, Greenlee rejected each of Posey's unreasonable demands. What's more, he prepared to swing back even harder against his bitter rival.

Confirming Posey's fears, Greenlee went to work bolstering his Crawfords team with more top talent. No player was off-limits, not even if he was technically signed to another team. And not even if that team was the Homestead Grays.

Greenlee's top recruit ahead of the 1932 season was a stocky twenty-one-year-old catcher and power hitter from Georgia named Josh Gibson. For everything Satchel Paige was on the mound, Gibson was that at the plate. He was fierce and imposing, as close to a sure thing as you could get in a fickle game like baseball, and because he'd been playing in and around Pittsburgh for the previous five years, local baseball fans were well aware of his talents. Indeed, signing Gibson was a club owner's dream. Even if fans couldn't name one other player on the field, they knew the slugger crouched behind home plate, and they showed up in

Josh Gibson, sometimes called the Black Babe Ruth, was a pure power hitter—and a source of contention between the dueling Cum Posey and Gus Greenlee.

droves to see him crush balls over the outfield fence.

Gibson had been a Homestead Gray for the 1930 and '31 seasons, but when Greenlee offered him $250 per month—$100 more than what Posey was paying him—he was happy to join the competition.

Gibson's signing drew harsh lines in Pittsburgh's battle for Black baseball supremacy, while also confirming one unavoidable truth: Greenlee may not have had the baseball know-how that Posey did, but whatever he lacked in experience he made up for in cold, hard cash. So flush was Greenlee that, by his second year as the Crawfords' owner, he had even broken ground on his own stadium—eponymous and self-financed. Though Greenlee, rightfully, had his critics, his stadium was still important in the world of Black baseball, a mark of necessary independence and a hopeful sign of things to come.

Greenlee Field opened on April 29, 1932, for a contest between the Crawfords and the New York Black Yankees. Paige pitched an outstanding game, striking out ten and giving up only six hits, but the Crawfords were unable to secure the win. Nonetheless, Greenlee's luck was still better than Posey's that year. Besides losing Gibson to the Crawfords and watching as Greenlee Stadium was constructed just blocks from Ammon Field, where the Grays played their home games, financial difficulties forced Posey to shutter his East-West League before the end of its first season.

Posey knew not to turn to his biggest competition for help with his crumbling organization, but even if he had, it wouldn't have mattered. Greenlee, always ready to loot an enemy's abandoned land, was ten steps ahead.

In the aftermath of Posey's failure, he decided to launch his own Black baseball league.

*** *

Ahead of the 1933 season, Greenlee gathered the owners from seven other teams, including Cum Posey of the Homestead Grays, to launch the new Negro National League. Like Rube Foster before him, Greenlee knew he couldn't build a successful league without the inclusion of the most outstanding teams in Black baseball.

Greenlee didn't have to like the Grays, but he couldn't deny their place among the best.

With fairness and costs in mind—given the ongoing Depression as well as the early collapse of Posey's East-West League—Greenlee, as NNL president, declared that home teams didn't have to promise a percentage of ticket sales to visiting clubs. He also demanded that player rosters be held to under $1,600 per month.

Today, Greenlee's insistence on a salary cap seems shocking, given his prior willingness to spend whatever was necessary to recruit top players. But it also shows his commitment to the league, as well as his desire to see all teams succeed.

With star players like Paige and Gibson, as well as promotional innovations like fan-voted All-Star game rosters, organized Black baseball was poised to be even more successful than it had been under Foster. And though Greenlee and Posey would continue their bitter rivalry until Greenlee left the Negro National League in 1939, their constant push to field the most competitive team— and to make money while doing it—benefited Black baseball as a whole. Players battled for spots on the most coveted rosters, and

Gus Greenlee didn't just sign the best Black baseball talent in the mid-1930s, including Hall of Famers Satchel Paige, Josh Gibson, and Oscar Charleston. He also built his baseball stadium, Greenlee Field, and was instrumental in launching the second Negro National League.

team owners paired those athletes with managers and coaches ready to polish their raw talent until it sparkled.

The Crawfords and Grays were, of course, just two of the clubs in the reborn Negro National League. There were others, too, including the Brooklyn Eagles.

Like Greenlee and Posey, the Manleys had their own ideas about how baseball teams and leagues should be run. After all, the years that lapsed between the end of Foster's league and the beginning of Greenlee's hadn't made the business of baseball any easier to navigate, especially for Black teams and executives.

It wouldn't be long before the owners realized that even a deep love for baseball and the Black community couldn't prevent struggle and conflict. And as Effa began to establish herself as an executive to be reckoned with—first within the Eagles organization and later within the NNL as a whole—she'd often find herself in the center of it all.

MAKING MOVES

By 1935, Greenlee's Negro National League was heading into its third season and already a much greater success than Posey's ill-fated East-West League. Besides the two Pittsburgh-area teams, there were clubs in Philadelphia, Newark, and Columbus, Ohio. And thanks to the Manleys' Brooklyn Eagles and Alex Pompez's New York Cubans, the NNL also had a permanent presence in America's baseball epicenter.

Before the start of the NNL's 1935 season, the Eagles headed south to Jacksonville, Florida, for spring training. Abe traveled with the team, and while there, he began writing Effa, asking her to help out with some of the club's front-office responsibilities.

"I suppose if we'd have been operating a long time and had some established help, he would have turned it over to them," Effa mentioned years later. "But little by little, I found myself doing more and more. I finally found myself completely involved."

Although Abe *(left)* funded the purchase of the Brooklyn Eagles, he quickly turned to Effa for help running the team.

During her career in baseball, Effa planned the Eagles' schedule, bought all the team's equipment, arranged travel for away games, and handled a host of other logistical tasks. Yet amid all the other front-office mayhem, there was one responsibility that Effa always considered a top priority, the work that could mean the difference between a prosperous season and a penniless one.

In the days before teams had entire staffs dedicated to marketing and promotions, Effa was a one-woman PR machine focused on gathering the support of the local community. The all-white Dodgers had been the only pro team based in Brooklyn, so when the Eagles arrived, Effa hoped that fans would come to their opening-day game, even if just to see whether the new Black team in town was worth all the fuss. Of course, Effa planned to put on a show so good that they'd come back again and again.

For the 1935 opening-day festivities at Ebbets Field, Effa staged an elaborate showcase. To kick things off, both teams marched from home plate to center field, serenaded by an all-Black marching band with a drum major at the helm. Next, New York Mayor Fiorella La Guardia threw out the first pitch, while other high-profile individuals, including Effa's boycott co-organizer Rev. John H. Johnson and representatives from the local media, looked on from box seats. It was a spectacle fit for a championship team; unfortunately, her players' performance failed to meet that standard.

First-inning home runs from left fielder Fats Jenkins and center fielder Rap Dixon put the Eagles ahead with a score of 4–1, but the Eagles didn't hold the lead long. The Grays answered with four runs in the top of the second inning and four more in the third. Effa, appalled by her team's inability to quench the Grays' smoking bats, went home to have a drink. "I never saw so many home runs in my life," she later said.

Jerry Benjamin, the Grays' center fielder, crushed any hopes of an Eagles comeback when he smashed a grand slam in the top of the fifth. Brooklyn did add one more run in the bottom of that inning, but it wasn't enough. All told, the Grays connected for twenty-three hits off four Eagles pitchers, amassing a final, embarrassing total of twenty runs. The Eagles scored only seven. From the beginning of the game until the end, the visiting Homestead Grays had played like the well-oiled pros they were, while Abe and Effa's roster of competitors' throwaways looked amateur at best.

Effa didn't want to lose an argument; she didn't want to lose a bet; and she certainly didn't want to lose a baseball game. But her team would, indeed, lose many more in 1935. After a couple of shake-ups—the Manleys replaced the Eagles' on-field manager and also brought in a couple of new players—the club was able to bounce back from its early drumming. But just barely. The Eagles finished the season in fifth place out of eight teams, with a winning percentage just above .500.

It is said there are no losses, only lessons, and Effa's inaugural season with the Eagles was a master class in sports business. For starters, Effa learned that she may have been cut out for baseball's front office after all, and with her team struggling on the field, she felt emboldened to take a more active role in the Eagles' on-the-field operations. The Eagles were just a month into the season when Effa, much as she had done during the meeting with William Blumstein, made her opinion known.

"[Abe] Manley met me in his apartment and offered me the manager's job," veteran first baseman George Giles later recalled. "He said, 'My wife wants you to manage the ball club.' He didn't say he wanted me. He said [his] wife wanted me."

In November 1935, after the Eagles' regular season ended, Effa also gained a thorough education in the workings of winter baseball leagues. She and Abe sponsored a team in the Puerto Rican league that played under the Brooklyn Eagles' name, even though the roster actually featured players from multiple Black teams.

Because of the warm weather and baseball's increasing popularity in Latin America, both Black and white players often traveled to Puerto Rico, Mexico, Cuba, and other countries during winter months to keep their form, and their wallets, in top condition. Effa took credit for, and pride in, that 1935 Puerto Rican tour—and not just because it provided the players with off-season employment and allowed her to broaden her influence as a real-deal baseball mogul. Above all else, Effa was a winner, and the team that represented the Eagles in Puerto Rico represented her well. They won the league championship and returned home with a gleaming, first-place trophy.

But of all the lessons Effa learned in 1935, the fact that she

After the 1935 season, Effa sponsored a Black team that played in Puerto Rico's Winter League and won this stunning trophy.

and Abe couldn't sustain a successful franchise in Brooklyn was perhaps the most important. Fan support was just too low, the competition for market share too high. Besides competing for fans with the New York Cubans of the Negro National League, the Eagles also had to contend with a slew of

New York–based semipro teams, as well as out-of-town clubs that visited in hopes of claiming their own chunk of the city's baseball profits.

Abe and Effa knew their situation was unlikely to improve in Brooklyn, but they also knew they weren't ready to leave the sport altogether. The only solution? They had to move.

Just across the Hudson River, Newark, New Jersey, felt like the perfect place for Abe and Effa to begin again for the 1936 season. The city was close enough to New York that any Brooklyn-based fans could easily make the trek to see the Eagles play; as an added bonus, the NNL's Newark Dodgers had already proved that the New Jersey town could support a Black baseball team. So when Abe discovered that Dodgers owner Charles Tyler was willing to turn over his entire team to Abe as payment for a $500 outstanding debt, the Manleys seized the opportunity. They merged the Brooklyn Eagles and Newark Dodgers teams and christened the new club as the Newark Eagles.

Even with visions of more fans and greater profits dancing in their heads, Abe and Effa knew they had their work cut out for them on the field. The Dodgers had fared even worse than the Eagles in '35, finishing the season at the very bottom of the NNL standings with an 18–43 record and a dismal .295 winning percentage. Still, the husband-and-wife team was confident. They were relocating to a market with less competition, and Effa was coming into her own as a capable baseball executive.

✳✳✳

Like New York, Chicago, and other cities across the country, Newark was effectively a segregated town. But even as unfair hiring practices, poor housing conditions, and subpar schools dogged Newark's Black community, its people were no victims. On the contrary, they embodied the same will and resilience that led Rube Foster, Gus Greenlee, and others to create their own opportunities in baseball when they weren't afforded any by whites. Indeed, the People's Finance Corporation, the Negro Funeral Directors of New Jersey, and the Black YMCA were just a few of the institutions that helped to promote Black pride and self-sufficiency in Newark while also combating the systemic racism of the time. This was the community that the Manleys pledged to support, and this was the community that the Manleys hoped would support them in return.

Newark's Black residents had limited funds to spend on amusement, and Effa's team competed with a thriving entertainment scene. There was a vaudeville theater in town, called the Orpheum, as well as numerous clubs that featured the biggest Black artists of the era. On any given night, the Black men and women of Newark could be found downtown, zoot-suited and grooving to the sounds of Cab Calloway, Lionel Hampton, Count Basie, and other performers.

To bridge this divide and attract some of the late-night crowd to the ballpark, Effa made every attempt to merge the worlds of sports and entertainment. She hosted musical performances during games and invited local celebrities to attend, much as she had done in Brooklyn. She also used the Eagles' platform to launch several charitable endeavors designed to boost ticket sales while also doing genuine good for the community.

During her time in Newark, Effa hosted a "Stop Lynching" campaign at Ruppert Stadium, selling buttons with the tagline to raise funds for the NAACP, of which she was a member and one-time treasurer of the New Jersey branch. She raised money for new medical equipment to be used at the Booker T. Washington Community Hospital, the city's only hospital to both treat and hire Black people. And via its Knothole Gang, the Eagles forged a lasting bond with the city's Black youth, allowing them free entry to games so they could see their diamond heroes up close.

As such, Newark's Black community returned Effa's affection with more of the same, welcoming her and Abe with open arms. But even as the Manleys got settled in New Jersey, their relationship with George Weiss, vice president of the minor-league Newark Bears, served as a sharp reminder of baseball's rigid color line.

Before moving the Eagles to Newark, Abe had finalized an agreement with Weiss that allowed the Eagles to play their home games at the Bears' Ruppert Stadium. The contract gave the Bears 20 percent of gross ticket revenue for all Eagles home games, while the visiting team took 30 percent. Out of the 50 percent that the Eagles kept, the Manleys had to pay for all services needed during the game, including ushers, ticket takers, and scoreboard operators. For night games, they paid an additional fee for stadium lighting.

The Eagles' arrangement, while fraught, was still fair, especially when compared with those of other Black teams that had no home field to speak of. Striking a deal directly with the stadium owner was certainly in the best interest of the Manleys, since scheduling games through a booking agent would have taken an even bigger slice out of the team's profits. Nonetheless, the Eagles' rental arrangement with the Bears represented the extent of the partnership between the two Newark-based teams.

According to historian James Overmyer, "the Eagles never played a single inning against what should have been their natural rivals [the Bears]," and it was largely because the Eagles had a better team.

No matter how much he stood to profit from a game against the Eagles, Weiss couldn't risk his all-white team losing to an all-Black team—not in front of people whose entire way of life depended on the notion that Black people, including Black baseball players, were second-class and second-best. He was more than willing to make money off Effa's club when they played in his stadium against other Black teams, but with his refusal to go head-to-head against the Eagles, Weiss proved that there was still a line that he—and other white baseball executives—would never cross.

TROUBLE IN PARADISE

Before their first season in Newark, Abe and Effa signed several talented men to their roster, including future Hall of Famers Ray Dandridge and Willie Wells, who were then considered the best in the Negro National League at third base and shortstop, respectively. By 1937, the Manleys had also added first baseman George "Mule" Suttles and second baseman Dick Seay, solidifying what became known as the "Million Dollar Infield." The moniker was a reference not to the players' actual salaries, but to the pay that Dandridge, Wells, Suttles, and Seay would have likely commanded had they been white and playing in the Majors.

Unfortunately, even the new and improved Eagles weren't

The first baseman of Newark's "Million Dollar Infield," Mule Suttles, is shown here at Ruppert Stadium, in a game against the New York Black Yankees.

enough to overtake the league-leading Homestead Grays. Committed to returning to the top of the Black baseball hierarchy, Cum Posey had brought on a business partner, a numbers banker named Rufus "Sonnyman" Jackson, in 1934. Posey may have wanted to keep his baseball business free of illegally gained funds, but he wanted to win even more. And with Jackson's cash at his disposal, Posey was able to rebuild his powerhouse club.

Effa longed to see the Eagles at the top of the Negro National League's standings, to usurp Posey as Black baseball's reigning ruler and crown herself queen. But it wasn't just the Grays' dominance that concerned her. Effa attended her first league meeting in January 1937 and quickly began establishing herself as a vocal leader among the NNL board members; at the same time, she learned how shaky Black baseball's foundation really was.

Before the '37 season began, controversy rocked the Negro National League when Satchel Paige, the NNL's charismatic celebrity and Gus Greenlee's cash cow, skipped out on his Crawfords contract. He'd taken off during the team's spring training and decided to play in the Dominican Republic. To make matters worse, he recruited nearly a dozen more of the Negro Leagues' top players to go with him.

⁂

Greenlee's Crawfords were training in New Orleans when Paige was approached by Dr. Jose Enrique Aybar, a dentist and deputy in the Dominican Republic congress. Aybar worked for Raphael Trujillo, the vicious Dominican dictator who wanted to use baseball to entertain his sports-loving subjects while distracting them from the atrocities of his regime. Trujillo wasn't much of a baseball fan himself, but if he was going to field a team in the Dominican summer league, it was going to be the best. And if his team, the Dragones, was going to be the best, it needed the best players.

Trujillo didn't have enough money to recruit the top white

players; even if he did, their ironclad contracts would have likely prevented any of them from leaving the United States during Major League Baseball's regular season. But the Negro Leaguers, with their paltry wages and tendency to jump contracts, seemed to be fair game.

Aybar knew that, of all the amazingly talented Black players who had been shut out of the Majors, Paige was in a class of his own. He saw Pittsburgh's hurler as the captain of Trujillo's roster, the principal around whom he could place a perfectly complementary cast. And just maybe, he thought, Paige would be willing to help lure those other players. All Aybar had to do was persuade the star pitcher to leave the Crawfords.

Satchel Paige (*top right*) was one of the biggest stars of Negro Leagues Baseball—so big, in fact, that he regularly organized his own barnstorming teams during the Negro Leagues off-season.

Paige was used to being recruited, to having wads of cash waved wildly in his face, but Aybar's proposal was like none he'd ever heard before. "We will give you thirty thousand American dollars for you and eight teammates," Aybar had said, "and you may take what you feel is your share and divide the rest."

Even if Paige had evenly split the money among himself and the other players, the $3,333 payday would have been worth it for three and a half months of work. Paige's reasoning that his salary should actually be twice the other players' made accepting Aybar's offer a no-brainer. As for the other players he recruited, including slugger Josh Gibson, they were all more than happy to trade their Negro Leagues salaries of a few hundred dollars per month to make a few thousand in the Dominican Republic.

Needless to say, the NNL owners were outraged.

* * *

In the United States, Negro Leaguers sought solace in their communities—in the all-Black neighborhoods where they lived and the Black-owned restaurants where they dined. As they took to the baseball field, those players were coached by Black men and cheered by Black fans; in many cases, their wages were paid by Black owners. Always, though, the race of those players was a hard-pumping undercurrent, the framework upon which every adverse aspect of their lives was built.

Those all-Black neighborhoods? Sometimes poor and decrepit, and nearly always created by government policies that prevented Black residents from living in close proximity to whites. The Black-owned restaurants? Born of necessity because Black patrons were refused entry and service at the whites-only cafes. And their Black coaches, fans, and team owners? They were in the same position as the players—making do with less but always hoping for more, forced to steer through the rough waters of oppression with a tight smile.

First baseman George Giles explained the extreme injustices that the Negro Leagues' players faced while barnstorming across the country, when the joys of baseball were shrouded by fear and uncertainty:

> We couldn't stay in white hotels; we couldn't eat in restaurants. In cities, there were usually Negro hotels. In those small towns, we would stay in family houses, two players here, two players there. Sometimes they'd fix us a meal in the colored church, or we'd bring out food from the

grocery store in a paper sack. If we were in Nebraska, we'd ride all night to Lincoln or Omaha. In some of those small towns we couldn't stay, and sometimes we'd just ride all night and sleep in the bus...

But it was just one of those things you learn to accept. You just roll with the punches. That was the way it was all over the country. See, we played all the states. Colorado was just as bad as Mississippi. New York was just as bad as Alabama. It was all the same.

It was different in Latin America, though. In places like Mexico, Cuba, and the Dominican Republic, Black baseball players were greeted by other Black and brown faces everywhere they went, from sunny beaches to food markets and, naturally, the ball field. Suddenly, they were no longer a minority, no longer subjected to second-class status. They were, instead, treated like heroes.

"The opportunities of a colored baseball player on these islands are the same or almost the same as those enjoyed by the white Major League players in the States," Paige wrote in an essay published in the *Afro-American* in July 1937. "That's something to think about."

So, of course, Paige was happy to play for Trujillo's Dragones. He was happier, still, to lead them to the Dominican championship, clinched during an eight-game series against the Águilas Cibaeñas of Santiago.

Meanwhile, back in America, the NNL owners fretted over how to handle the pitcher and his contract-jumping comrades. Gus Greenlee was facing financial distress—police had recently raided his numbers racket—and the defection of his best players left him in a particularly perilous situation. Still, as the president of the NNL, he appeared to take a hard stance against the jumpers not long after they left for the Caribbean.

"If they fail to report to their clubs by Saturday, May 15, they will be barred from organized baseball for one year and fined," Greenlee said. "Furthermore, no league club will play in any park where outlaw ball-players appear."

On May 25, the NNL took further steps to secure the return of the rogue players by having Ferdinand Morton, the part-time commissioner of the league, send a telegram to Democratic Senator

Robert Wagner of New York. On behalf of the owners, Morton argued that the players had been illegally coerced by the Dominican government and that the American government should step in and demand that they be sent home.

When that didn't work, Ira Hurwick, a white attorney representing Greenlee's Crawfords, agreed to accompany several NNL owners, including Effa, to Washington, DC. For three hours, they met with the head of the Division of American Republics and tried to persuade him to reclaim their wayward stars. In the end, their efforts proved futile. The American government declared the matter a private one that the Dominican government was unlikely to get involved in. More important, Hurwick admitted that, because of the flimsy nature of Negro Leagues contracts, the players were not liable for any damages in breaking their agreements.

Since 1879, Major League Baseball had included a reserve clause in all its contracts, which stipulated that the signing team controlled the rights to a player for the entirety of his career, unless the team waived, sold, or traded the player to another club. This prevented players from jumping to another team—and promised legal consequences if they did.

While Major Leaguers were known to play in Latin America

during the winter months, the reserve clause kept them stateside in the summer, during the MLB's regular season. But the Negro Leagues' contracts contained no such stipulation.

Left to their own defenses, the NNL owners agreed to fine Paige, Gibson, and the other players $200, which was to be paid before they could join an NNL roster for the 1938 season. The owners also refused to reinstate them for the remainder of the 1937 season when they finally did return to the United States in late July. But the players, riding high off their Dominican victory and flush with cash, weren't concerned. Led by Paige, they formed their own team, the Santo Domingo All-Stars, and barnstormed across the western United States.

✳✳✳

If nothing else, the events of 1937 revealed the instability of the Negro Leagues and the tendency for its key members to place personal concerns ahead of the group's. Indeed, the NNL bosses soon discovered that Greenlee had actually encouraged the Santo Domingo All-Stars tour and helped to promote some of their games. This was in direct violation of the owners' agreement, but also not surprising. Presumably, the still struggling Greenlee traded his involvement with the All-Stars for a cut of the profits.

Effa, still relatively new to the world of professional baseball, was appalled by the chaos. She expected competition from her colleagues, but she hadn't realized how much foreign teams, and even the players themselves, would threaten her business. Yet she remained undeterred, and instead of fixating on all that was wrong with Black baseball, Effa decided to focus on its promise. It was a promise shaped by diamond stars like Paige and Gibson, players whose talents shone like glittery jewels, so remarkable that men like Trujillo were willing to dig deep into their pockets to attract them.

Despite the drama of 1937, Effa had no reason to give up on Black baseball, for an infinite future still seemed to lay ahead. Back then, Effa had no way of knowing what she would eventually learn—that the challenges she and the other owners faced would persist for more than a decade longer, choking Black baseball until it drew its last breath.

SPEAKING UP

As the summer of 1937 wore on, the Negro National League's leadership remained fractured. Greenlee's support of the Santo Domingo All-Stars only deepened his feud with Homestead Grays owner Cum Posey, and thanks to his regular column in the *Pittsburgh Courier*—courtesy of his father's investment in the Black newspaper—Posey could air the NNL's dirty laundry before a wide audience.

"The writer of this column, who as all the readers know, is an executive of the Homestead Grays, took the liberty the past week to write [Gus Greenlee,] the President of the Negro National League and request that he resign from the office of president," Posey wrote on August 14. "This year, the league has gone along like a ship without a rudder."

The NNL may have been rudderless, but, as one of her earliest allies, Posey did acknowledge Effa's successful acclimation into the world of professional baseball, as well as her earliest pushes to improve the league's operations. He even took to his *Courier* column to offer public praise:

> Mrs. Abe Manley, who is rapidly learning the business end of the baseball game, addressed the members and in no uncertain terms expressed her disapproval of [the] way the members conducted league business with the wonderful future possible for Negro baseball if conducted in a businesslike manner.

Posey was so impressed with Effa's business acumen that he—along with each of the remaining NNL owners except Greenlee—voted to send Effa to Chicago in early August 1937 to represent the league's financial interests at the East-West Classic. Since 1933, the same year Major League Baseball hosted its inaugural All-Star game, the Classic had served as Black baseball's star-studded version. In the process, it had become one of the most profitable events on the Negro Leagues' calendar.

The Classic was birthed when two sportswriters discussed the idea for a Black All-Star game with Cum Posey, proposing that the contest be played at Yankee Stadium in New York. Later, when the writers mentioned their idea to Greenlee—and told him Posey was involved—the Crawfords owner took over the planning and moved the game to Chicago's Comiskey Park. Greenlee enlisted the help of Tom Wilson, owner of the Nashville Elite Giants, and Robert Cole, owner of the Chicago American Giants, to launch

Launched in 1934, the East-West All-Star Classic drew tens of thousands of Black baseball fans to Chicago's Comiskey Park to see the best Negro Leagues players take the field. Here, pitcher Willie Foster is recognized for his prowess during the inaugural contest.

the storied event, but the greatest financial risk fell squarely on his shoulders. Greenlee even put up $2,500 of his own money to pay Comiskey's rental fees.

Over the years, the East-West Classic grew into an amazing extravaganza, thanks largely to Greenlee's efforts. Not only did the game showcase the finest Black baseball players, as voted on by the fans, but, like the Negro World Series of the 1920s, it also helped Black baseball to more closely resemble organized white baseball. While Major League Baseball's All-Star Game pitted the finest players from the American League against the top National Leaguers, the East-West Classic was a yearly showdown between the best of the eastern-based Negro National League and the most talented players from midwestern Black teams.

There was trouble amid the success, though. In 1934, just its second year in operation, nearly thirty thousand fans attended the Classic, reportedly the largest crowd ever at a Black sporting event. But despite the strong attendance in '34 and '35, Posey felt that some of the NNL clubs weren't getting a fair cut of the profits and accused Greenlee of skimming funds off the top.

In his defense, Greenlee argued that he deserved a larger cut because he'd helped to develop the contest and remained one of its key organizers. In 1936, when Commissioner Morton and several of the other NNL owners tried to bypass Greenlee and move the game to New York, he stood firm then, too, refusing to relinquish his authority. "When no one had any faith in the idea [of staging the Classic], it was perfectly all right for us to gamble with our money," Greenlee said in response. "But after its success had been assured, we were sorta shunted out of the picture."

The Classic remained in Chicago, but ahead of the 1937 showdown, Posey and the other eastern bosses wanted a guarantee that the game's profits would be fairly distributed. So they asked Effa to review the financial arrangements of the game with the stipulation that, if the conditions were not satisfactory, the owners who felt shortchanged would bar their players from taking the field.

While Posey felt confident in Effa's presence at Comiskey, noting that she "handled the affairs in a capable manner and gave each member an important financial report of the game," Greenlee objected wildly. "The proper place for women is by the fireside and not functioning in positions to which their husbands have been elected," he said.

Unfortunately for Greenlee, his call for Effa to stick to her wifely duties went unheeded. She and Abe were already at work on their next big project.

Just ahead of the 1937 season, Major Robert R. Jackson, a Black politician from Chicago, brought together eight Black teams from across the Midwest and South—including the Kansas City Monarchs, Chicago American Giants, and Memphis Red Sox—to form the Negro American League (NAL). For the first time since 1929, there were two professional Negro Leagues, and fans across the country had access, once again, to Black baseball of the highest quality. On one hand, the NAL presented direct competition for the eastern-based NNL; on the other, it revealed a fantastic opportunity.

Effa saw the return of the Negro World Series as the natural next step for Black baseball, one that would further legitimize the revitalized Negro Leagues. She also believed that the Series could be a valuable moneymaking opportunity for participating teams. Because the Black community as a whole had yet to rebound from the Great Depression, many Negro Leagues teams struggled to break even. Most operated in the red.

But Greenlee rejected the idea that proceeds from a Negro World Series should be used to bolster the lagging finances of individual clubs. He felt that any revenue earned by an NNL team in the Series should be added to the league treasury; he also believed that the Series was "nothing more than a personal promotion" organized by Posey and the Manleys. According to Greenlee, this, along with Effa's East-West involvement, was proof that "the owners of the clubs in the Negro National League [were] interested only in themselves and their own selfish motives." Interestingly, Greenlee also said that if the Series was, indeed, a "league" promotion—and not simply a side hustle of three individual owners—then he, as the NNL president, should get 10 percent of the proceeds.

In an open letter published in the *Pittsburgh Courier*, Greenlee accused Abe and Effa of repeatedly "overstep[ping] their bounds" and threatened to remove the Eagles from the NNL for the 1938 season. "Just who the members of the League will be, I do not know at present," he wrote, "but I do know however that any club affiliated with the League next year will abide by the rules that govern the League and will not endeavor to usurp the authority or ignore the position of this office."

***

Dissension was threatening to tear the Negro National League apart, but that didn't change the fact that Effa still had a job to do, one that she would later say was one of the most "difficult and exasperating jobs in the world." Effa conducted all the Eagles' business affairs, and during the economically volatile 1930s, this was arguably the most important role within any Black baseball club.

Game to game and season to season, keeping the Newark Eagles on the baseball diamond required tremendous costs. From purchasing uniforms and cleats to paying for promotional expenses, Effa estimated that the Eagles' total cost of operations during the five-month Negro National League season was around $40,000, the equivalent of more than $700,000 today. Meanwhile, to keep fans coming to games—financially strapped Black fans, especially—ticket prices had to be kept low.

In 1939, adult tickets were forty cents for bleacher seats, fifty-nine cents for the grandstand, and seventy-seven cents for a box seat; for children under twelve, tickets were fifteen cents for the bleachers and twenty-five cents for the grandstand.

Receipts from a game held on August 20 showed that a total paid attendance of 929 resulted in gross sales of $503.23. After the visiting team's 30 percent share, equaling $150.97, and the Newark Bears' 20 percent cut of $100.65 for the use of the stadium, the Eagles were left with $251.61. Subtracting the salaries of police officers and ticket sellers, along with other operating costs, resulted in net profits of just $176.83 for the home team.

That season, the Eagles played fifty-nine games. Assuming an average profit of $200 for each contest—though attendance fluctuated and the team made less when playing on the road—Newark would have netted just $11,800 on the season. That's far less than the $40,000 Abe and Effa would have needed to simply break even.

Money was always tight in Black baseball, sure, but Effa was committed to presenting the Eagles as a well-run franchise all the same. "We were proud of the fact that players from the Newark Eagles' organization never were forced to wait for their paychecks," Effa wrote in her memoir, *Negro Baseball…Before Integration*. "Paydays were the first and fifteenth of every month during the season, and we diligently met this deadline promptly, in all instances."

Effa and Abe invested a lot in their players, via salaries and their athletic development, and they felt it only fair to expect the best in return. Johnny Davis, an outfielder and pitcher who played for the Eagles in the forties, explained:

Effa had an apartment house on Crawford Street, and she'd get you down there and, boy, she'd blast you. Maybe you didn't have clean white socks on your uniform, or you looked sloppy on the field, or your shirt was torn and "I didn't like the way you did this."

What could you say? You'd sit there, and after she was all through, say, "Aaaah."

Well, you're representing something in Newark. You walk down the street, you had to look, not like a bum, you had to look halfway decent. You can't blame her for that.

Because she was determined to present the Newark Eagles as a model franchise and knew that her players would often be unfairly judged by their appearance, Effa demanded that her team look their best at all times.

Effa couldn't change the fact that Black players and teams were relegated to separate baseball fields, the victims of unyielding racism. But she could present the Newark Eagles as a premier ball club, one comprising talented, upstanding men, one that was no different from the best Major League teams.

If the Eagles' players represented Effa and the city of Newark, it could similarly be argued that the Negro National League team owners represented the entire Black community. But Effa couldn't control the other owners' behaviors or decisions. Nor could she force them to settle disputes in-house, away from the prying eyes of the public.

Integration was far from a foregone conclusion in the late 1930s, but as the decade came to a close and international injustices cast a spotlight on America's persistent flaws, change was beginning to appear on the horizon. This change brought analysis and introspection, and it wasn't just Major League Baseball that would have to address its deep-seated issues.

The Negro Leagues would have to as well.

WAGING WAR

Ever since the "gentleman's agreement" of 1887, organized white baseball had successfully barred Black players from joining its ranks. For the most part, Black and white athletes were forced to circle their own, distinct orbits. Baseball fans, on the other hand, faced no such constraints. White fans were often seen at Negro Leagues contests, and Black fans happily attended the games of their favorite Major Leaguers.

The reality of integrated fan bases had a major impact on the business of white baseball. Interestingly, Major League bosses who were vigilant in upholding baseball's color line were also happy to capitalize on the support of Black fans. This had been the way of the baseball world for years, after all, and there was no reason to believe that anything would ever change.

No reason, that is, until a 1938 incident began to reveal the irreconcilable conflict between the intentions of Major League owners and the desires of their diverse followers.

✳ ✳ ✳

Before the 1936 World Series, New York Yankee left fielder Jake Powell was a relative unknown on a lineup boasting Hall of Fame greats Joe DiMaggio and Lou Gehrig. That all changed during the Series, however, when Powell's bat introduced him to the world. He finished with ten hits, eight runs, four walks, and a .455 batting average—a stat line that led all players on either team and lifted the Yankees to their fifth World Series title.

Two years later, Powell's name was again on the lips of everyone in baseball. But this time, it was for a much different reason.

On the afternoon of Friday, July 29, 1938, just before the Yankees were set to face the White Sox in a road game at Comiskey Park, Chicago radio announcer Bob Elson stepped into the visiting team's dugout to capture some B-roll, perhaps some light banter with a player that would keep listeners engaged before the real action started. Elson found Powell there, prepping for the 2:00 PM start time, and decided to interview him.

"How do you keep trim during the winter months in order to keep up your batting average?" Elson asked the outfielder.

It was a softball of a question, fat and hanging over the heart of the plate. Powell could have driven it in any direction, yet the budding star flailed wildly, missing the pitch entirely—albeit intentionally. "Oh, that's easy," Powell said with a smirk. "I'm a policeman, and I beat n——rs over the head with my blackjack."

Like sailors rushing to plug a boat's hole before it capsizes, WGN, the radio network hosting Elson, quickly cut the interview. Suddenly, there was only stillness over the airwaves, a deafening silence after Powell's earsplitting slur. But it was too late. Tens of thousands of people had heard the racist remarks, including many Black Chicagoans whose fandom wasn't limited to the Chicago American Giants and other local Black teams.

Angry listeners called the station to denounce Powell's statement, and the next day, a group of Chicago's Black leaders showed up at Comiskey to present a petition that called for him to be banned from the Majors for the rest of his career. The uproar was swift and loud, like nothing baseball had ever seen before.

When New York Yankee outfielder Jake Powell forced the issue of Major League Baseball's color line to the center of public conversation, MLB commissioner Kenesaw Mountain Landis (*pictured*) could no longer avoid taking a stance.

Commissioner Landis stopped short of condemning Powell's bigotry and even sought to minimize the backlash by describing the remarks as "an uncomplimentary reference to a portion of the population." Landis also ignored calls to permanently ban Powell, choosing, instead, to suspend him for ten games.

For the Black community, Landis's response was welcome, but perhaps not fully sufficient. If nothing else, his attempts to make amends for Powell's racism illuminated a pressing issue that the league had continued to willfully ignore.

It would be years before Major League Baseball would take tangible steps to rectify its ungentlemanly hypocrisy. But in the wake of Powell's suspension, many in the Black community speculated about what Landis's action could mean for Black baseball players. Wendell Smith of the *Pittsburgh Courier* was convinced that the commissioner had at least unlatched a gate that had previously been chained shut. It was up to his people, then, to swing it wide open.

In the January 14, 1939, edition of his "Smitty's Sports Spurts" column, Smith wrote:

> The big league moguls realize the value of the Negro dollar . . . And as a result, they treat us with care and caution. They give us interviews and hope in regards to the major league color question. They are careful not to let us think they don't give a hoot about us . . .
>
> In these days of world unrest, while our great President is standing on high and crying of the inhuman practices being carried on in other countries and shouting his political lungs out about freedom and democratic ideals, we feel that this is the time for Negroes the nation over to organize and fight for the Negro ball player. If we must, we should show Hitler and the rest of the world that compared with Uncle Sam, he's not really so bad after all. The only difference is that his methods are a bit cruder.

Smith's remark about the Nazi leader being "not so bad" when compared with the US government spoke to the feelings of millions of Black people across the country, both in and out of baseball. With the nation on the brink of World War II, Americans were rightly concerned about the persecution of Jews in Europe. But what about the daily injustices faced by their fellow Black citizens at home?

Smith closed his column by suggesting that the Black community form an organization similar to the NAACP that would fight for the integration of Major League Baseball "until we drop from exhaustion."

"We have been unable to make any progress fighting as individuals," he added, "but united into one large group we can bring pressure to bear and receive the consideration we have been demanding for so long."

While noble in their intention, Smith's comments unfortunately discounted the immeasurable time and money that Negro Leagues executives had been investing into Black baseball players for decades. Indeed, the Black community already had an organization that was well positioned to address the matter of baseball's integration...

If only its leaders could get on one accord.

ENEMIES AND ALLIES

Tensions between Negro National League owners came to a head during the annual league meeting in February 1940, when Effa, Abe, and the owners of the New York Cubans and New York Black Yankees moved to have C. B. Powell, publisher of the *New York Amsterdam News*, installed as the NNL's new president.

Despite playing a vital role in the development of the new NNL and serving as its president for several years, Gus Greenlee was on the back side of a striking descent from Black baseball's pinnacle. His finances never fully recovered from police raids on his numbers operation and the desertion of his best players during the 1937 season; by 1938, the city of Pittsburgh had assumed ownership of his lauded Greenlee Field and made plans to demolish it. For a while, Greenlee seemed more focused on the boxers he was managing, including light heavyweight champion John Henry Lewis, than his faltering baseball business. But in January 1939, Lewis suffered a knockout in an important match the day after Greenlee's brother was killed in a car accident. With no other option, the Crawfords' owner resigned from his position as NNL president in February and disbanded his team two months later.

Tom Wilson, who remained based in Nashville even though his Elite Giants team had moved to Baltimore, took over in Greenlee's stead. Wilson was nothing like the combative Greenlee, but Effa didn't see his amicable nature as an inherent positive. She wanted a president who was bold enough to push back against the outside interests that threatened to further erode Black baseball's minimal profits—namely, white booking agents.

Decades after Nat Strong first assumed control of Black baseball's bookings—and even years after his death—Negro Leagues team owners still relied on booking agents to secure rentals of Yankee Stadium and other profitable venues in the New York market. In 1937, the NNL had agreed to give William Leuschner, former partner of Nat Strong, and Ed Gottlieb, co-owner of the

Philadelphia Stars, 10 percent of proceeds to book any independent games for league teams. But three years later—and despite the fact that 25 percent of the agents' total take went back into the NNL's treasury—Effa and some of the other owners were beginning to resent the amount of control that Leuschner and Gottlieb exerted.

On the matter of the white booking agents, the NNL was split along geographical lines. Effa and Abe sided with James Semler, owner of the New York Black Yankees, and Alex Pompez of the New York Cubans. Despite having no official home ballpark, Semler's and Pompez's teams played the majority of their games in New York

In the 1930s, Yankee Stadium and other New York venues represented the most lucrative playing opportunities for Negro Leagues teams. They were also all controlled by white booking agents who took a cut of profits.

and, thus, stood to lose the most money to booking fees. On the other side of the aisle stood Wilson, Cum Posey of the Homestead Grays, and Ed Bolden.

After spending two decades with the Hilldale Daisies, Bolden left the club in 1930 and remained on the sideline for a couple of years; when Bolden did return to Black baseball in 1932, he partnered with Ed Gottlieb to found the Philadelphia Stars. Bolden was roundly criticized for entering into a fifty-fifty agreement with the booking agent, but much as he had done when Rube Foster questioned his alliance with Nat Strong in 1923, Bolden justified his actions. Given Gottlieb's grasp on the Philly baseball market, Bolden saw the cooperative as the only way to field a profitable team.

One of Effa's biggest complaints about Negro National League operations was the continued reliance on booking agents like Eddie Gottlieb, who charged a 10 percent fee to book Black baseball games in some white-owned stadiums.

Effa wanted Wilson to step in and disentangle Gottlieb and other booking agents from NNL profits, but he wouldn't do it. With the nickname "Smiling" Tom, Wilson's personality likely played a role in his reluctance to address the issue; Effa also knew that Wilson and his Baltimore Elite Giants profited from relationships with Leuschner and Gottlieb. With that in mind, Effa moved to nominate a president who, like officials of the white Major Leagues, had no team affiliations. But as the debate over who would be named NNL president for the 1940 season wore on during the league meeting, tempers flared.

Posey took a firm stance on behalf of the booking agents, declaring that they more than earned their fees and actually saved teams money. "The promoter ... does get ten per cent of NET receipts," he later wrote in the *Courier*. "This promoter puts up all advance money for the park. He assumes all liability insurance at a cost of twenty-five dollars—the liability insurance formerly cost $183 each game. This promoter gets Yankee Stadium for the league clubs for $1,000; the cost up until last year was $3,500. This promoter cut the operating expenses for each game from $2,000 a game to $1,000 per game."

Posey's points may have been valid, but finances were only a minor concern for Effa. "We are fighting for something bigger than a little money!" she exclaimed during the meeting. "We are fighting for a race issue."

Effa's decision to draw a color line in the middle of the NNL's winter meeting didn't go over well, especially since Gottlieb, who was white, was in attendance. When he later wrote about the meeting in the *Courier*, Posey jumped to Gottlieb's aid, noting that it was hypocritical for Effa to make such a statement when each of the other owners had, at one point or another, been the sole Black person in a room full of white people. Posey also mentioned that, in September 1939, Effa had staged a four-game exhibition at Ruppert Stadium and collected 10 percent of the proceeds for herself.

Back at the meeting, the conversation was continuing to spiral out of control. Not only did Effa refuse to retreat from her position, but she also called Posey a handkerchief head, a derogatory term used to refer to Black people who are accused of abandoning their own race in an attempt to ally with whites, often for their own personal gain.

Disgusted, and with the presidential vote deadlocked at 3–3, Posey boldly declared that he wasn't going to return until Effa was back "where she belongs—in the kitchen." According to his *Courier* column, Effa's behavior had been a "disgusting exhibition for a lady."

Certainly, Effa's reaction to Posey was unprofessional, inappropriate, and disrespectful. But her intent—to bring attention to the ironclad control that a handful of white men held over Black base-ball's most lucrative affairs—was nonetheless important. When he launched the first Negro National League in 1920, Rube Foster desired to build an organization that was free of white involvement and influence. He hadn't been able to achieve that, and two decades later, Black baseball was still struggling to stand on its own.

* * *

As Wendell Smith and others raised the question of integration in Major League Baseball, Effa worried that white booking agents weren't fully invested in the future of Black baseball, or in position-ing the NNL to take advantage of the rapidly changing times. How could they be? she wondered. They didn't come from the commu-nities that birthed Negro Leagues Baseball. They didn't understand the hurt and pain that seized the hearts of Black men, women, and children, or how the athletic prowess that grew out of that pain loosened its clutch just a bit.

And from a purely financial perspective, white booking agents, on the whole, hadn't invested the tens of thousands of dollars into Black baseball that the NNL owners had. They hadn't scoured small towns and big cities for top talent, developing it and leverag-ing it to build teams so good that they rivaled the white ones;

neither were they losing money year after year but still refusing to fold. The agents didn't understand what Black baseball teams meant to Black kids who could watch their heroes smash home runs and dig ground balls out of the dirt, heroes who looked just like them.

Effa may not have been fixated on the money that the agents were making in exchange for their booking services, but she did believe that money was their primary motivator. She believed that even Gottlieb, who had invested his own money into the Philadelphia Stars team, was only involved in Negro Leagues Baseball because of the potential paycheck it represented. Effa was incensed that Posey couldn't see that.

✳✳✳

As the 1940 season approached, there was a war within the Negro National League, to be sure. Still, it was nothing like the conflict that loomed ahead. With Japan's attack on Pearl Harbor on December 7, 1941, the country was plunged into the Second World War and forced to deal with the ugliest parts of the human spirit, both at home and abroad.

And, as Wendell Smith had predicted, baseball was pushed to the front line.

PART III

A Change Is Gonna Come

BATTLE WOUNDS

Even before the United States officially joined World War II, the country's economy was on the upswing. Suddenly, men and women who had been out of work since the Depression were being recruited to manufacture the weapons and ammunition needed to sustain a global conflict. This pre-war industrial boom was good news for the nation as a whole, and it was even better news for many white families still struggling to make ends meet. But for other families— Black families, in particular—finances remained tight.

In 1933, before Hitler and his Nazi forces invaded Poland, President Franklin Delano Roosevelt instituted a series of reforms called the New Deal. The New Deal was designed to counteract the lingering effects of the Great Depression, but as it failed to overcome the nation's prejudices, white families benefited most and Black families were, inevitably, left behind.

The Federal Housing Authority, developed to provide a path to homeownership for all Americans, refused to guarantee loans for Black buyers who wanted to purchase homes in predominantly white neighborhoods. Meanwhile, the National Recovery Administration, which set minimum wages and maximum work hours for employees, actually led to the firing of half a million Black workers when their employers deemed them unworthy of the NRA-mandated benefits.

The National Recovery Administration, designed to get Americans back to work and institute fair hiring practices, had the opposite effect in many Black communities.

Yet even as the New Deal continued to reinforce economic inequality, Black leaders still believed that America's involvement in World War II would bring great opportunity to their community. Sure enough,

America's entry into battle changed everything. When the country's labor demand increased overnight, employers could no longer afford to discriminate. Consequently, Black families that were still mired in the thick residue of the Depression suddenly had more than enough—to pay rent, to feed their kids, and even to attend a baseball game.

The problem was, as the 1942 season approached, no one could be sure whether their beloved game would continue during the war. Was it patriotic to pursue such trivial pursuits in the midst of a global crisis?

In a letter to Kenesaw Mountain Landis dated January 15, 1942, President Roosevelt answered that question with a resounding *yes*. With war raging abroad, he told Major League Baseball's commissioner, America needed the sport more than ever:

> *I honestly feel that it would be best for the country to keep baseball going. There will be fewer people unemployed and everybody will work longer hours and harder than ever before.*

And that means that they ought to have a chance for recreation and for taking their minds off their work even more than before…

Here is another way of looking at it—if 300 teams use 5,000 or 6,000 players, these players are a definite recreational asset to at least 20,000,000 of their fellow citizens—and that in my judgment is thoroughly worthwhile.

Roosevelt's announcement generated excitement among fans who would still be able to watch their favorite teams battle on the baseball diamond, as well as Major League team owners who could keep the turnstiles spinning during the war. Meanwhile, in the Negro Leagues, spirits were even higher. Now that Black wallets were filled with a little more cash, owners of Black teams were poised to finally see a return on their years and years of investment.

✳✳✳

As with any conflict, war separates winners from losers, and it is no exaggeration to say that Negro Leagues Baseball was one of the greatest victors of World War II. But even as ticket sales soared, allowing owners to raise prices and rake in greater profits, challenges remained.

Both the Majors and the Negro Leagues lost players who were shipped overseas to fight. Black baseball faced an additional hurdle, however, when players considered abandoning their roster sports in favor of more lucrative factory jobs. Black baseball players had never made as much as white players, but before the war years, they were at least guaranteed to make more than the Black men forced to work in menial, unskilled positions. Then the war came and opened up opportunities for manufacturing work, and Black baseball owners—despite increased profits—couldn't quite compete. At the same time, those owners were also struggling to get their business affairs in order, as members from the broader Black community continued to publicize the Negro Leagues' flaws.

According to Buster Miller, writer for the *New York Age*, "the chief weakness of organized Negro baseball" was the lack of regular reporting of game results. "When players like [Josh] Gibson, [Ed] Stone, [Buck] Leonard, and others now active, hang up their spikes at the end of their respective careers, who is to say just how effective or valuable they were," Miller added. "Surely not the records, because [...] there aren't any records kept."

Today, much of what we know about the Negro Leagues comes from the archives of Black newspapers like the *Pittsburgh Courier* and *Chicago Defender*. They published Negro Leagues scores and updates when white papers had no interest; in addition to serving as the official record for league standings, these updates also provided the only way for fans to keep up with their favorite teams and players.

Effa understood the importance of accurate reporting and had long pushed the other owners to report their scores immediately after contests. In early 1939, she even helped to create a process that would simplify reporting across the NNL.

After each weekday or Saturday game, the home team was required to send the score, by innings, to Ed Gottlieb. Not only was Gottlieb a booking agent for Negro Leagues games and co-owner of the Philadelphia Stars, but he also served as the Negro National League's co-secretary that season. Gottlieb's office was closed Sundays and holidays, though, so if games were played on those days, home teams were asked to send their results to Effa. Finally, full details of each week's games were to be sent by the following Thursday to Cum Posey, the Homestead Grays owner and the NNL's second secretary.

Representing the final step of the reporting process, Posey

was to ensure that all game results were published in a timely fashion, but Effa soon realized that he was the most significant hindrance to the entire process. She said as much in a May 26 letter to Chester Washington, the *Courier*'s sports editor, while also delivering corrected scores from the previous week's game:

> *It seems ridiculous that you should get this information in this way from me, as the League has two secretaries, one in Phila and one in Pittsburgh...*

> *We had devised a plan this year by which I believe results could have been handled very satisfactory [sic], but we were unable to get the co-operation of all the Clubs, mainly the Grays...*

> *I do not know what Posey's objection could be in refusing, unless it is that he wants to have the results handled by him in case the race is close and he might be able to do a little juggling. Why any one [sic] should object to the newspapers getting this information properly, I cannot understand.*

Speaking of the incomprehensible, Effa also couldn't understand why the Negro National League owners had yet to elect a neutral president to lead them—someone who, unlike the Baltimore Elite Giants' Tom Wilson, didn't have ties to one of the teams. Even after the drama of the 1940 NNL winter meeting, Wilson had managed to retain his title for both the 1940 and '41 seasons. Abe and Effa hoped things would be different in 1942, however, so they nominated Judge Joseph Rainey for president. Hailing from Pennsylvania, Rainey was a man who had extensive sports experience and who, in Effa's estimation, was "a Negro ... interested in the future of his race."

Abe didn't vote in the presidential election, and Effa, without an official league title, was not allowed to. Alas, all others in attendance voted to reelect Wilson. It was a blow so significant that Abe and Effa threatened to leave the NNL and operate their team independently. It was only a brief consideration, however, and with the beginning of the '42 season looming and the war raging on, the Manleys decided to stick around, effecting change when they could and striving for acceptance when they couldn't.

Ultimately, of all the challenges Abe and Effa faced during that time, the persistent calls for integration proved the most formidable of all. As Black men and women joined the effort to fight for the lives and liberties of millions of Europeans, many questioned why they weren't afforded the same freedoms at home.

This sentiment applied to all areas of work and life, and baseball was no exception.

* * *

As a sportswriter for the *Pittsburgh Courier,* Wendell Smith was a vocal advocate for the integration of the Majors. He believed that Black athletes were every bit as talented as white ones. In 1939, he had decided to ask key members of Major League Baseball teams whether they agreed. When white teams came to Pittsburgh to play against the Pirates during the 1939 season, Smith met them at the Schenley Hotel. Notepad and pen in hand, he'd corner players and managers alike and ask them, "Have you ever seen any Negro ballplayers who you think could play in the Major Leagues?"

The results of Smith's informal poll were striking: About three-quarters of the men he interviewed—including superstars like Dizzy Dean, Honus Wagner, and Mel Ott—spoke highly of Black players and supported their entry into Major League Baseball.

Emboldened, Smith published his findings to wide acclaim. In

Writing for the *Pittsburgh Courier* newspaper, Wendell Smith used his pen to push for racial progress, most notably with a 1939 series of articles that revealed that white players and managers were actually open to the integration of the Major Leagues.

revealing the true feelings of some of the most influential men in white baseball, he had exposed the first crack in Major League Baseball's color line. And soon enough, that crack branched off into countless other fissures, each growing in size and strength as more reporters began asking similar questions. In an interview with Lester Rodney of the *Daily Worker* newspaper, Brooklyn Dodgers manager Leo Durocher even said that he would be happy to coach a Black player "if the bosses said it was all right."

As the collective conversation around baseball's integration continued to escalate, it eventually reached the office of Major League Baseball's commissioner, Kenesaw Mountain Landis. For most of his tenure, Landis had evaded any discussion of race in America's pastime. After all, he'd been hired to clean up the sport after the Black Sox Scandal of 1919, in which the Chicago White

Sox allegedly lost the World Series on purpose in exchange for payouts from sports gamblers. Bringing Black players into Major League Baseball wasn't on his list of job responsibilities.

Historians question whether Landis was truly an avowed racist, but we do know that, if nothing else, Landis was fully invested in maintaining the status quo. Segregation had been in place long before he became commissioner, and because he was kept busy with other matters, Landis likely believed that he was doing the right thing by remaining silent about integration. But come 1942, he could remain silent no more.

On May 6, the *Daily Worker* published an open letter from Rodney to Landis that quoted Durocher's 1939 comments and took the commissioner to task for allowing baseball's continued exclusion of Black players. Soon thereafter, Landis called a closed-door meeting with Durocher, presumably to chastise him for implying that Black athletes were intentionally being kept out of the Majors. Though Landis was reluctant to address the matter directly, he didn't want Durocher's comments to create a public perception that Major League Baseball was still rife with bad behavior.

After the meeting, Landis made his first public statement on the matter:

Certain managers in organized baseball have been quoted as saying the reason Negroes are not playing in organized baseball is [that the] commissioner would not permit them to do so. Negroes are not barred from organized baseball by the commissioner and never have been during the 21 years I have served. There is no rule in organized baseball prohibiting their participation and never has been to my knowledge. If Durocher, any other manager, or all of them, want to sign one, or twenty-five Negro players, it is all right with me. That is the business of the managers and the club owners. The business of the commissioner is to interpret the rules of baseball and enforce them.

Landis's remarks signaled a breakthrough for Black players who'd been waiting their entire lives to join the ranks of Ruth and Gehrig. But it was also a bit of a nonstatement. Landis didn't erase baseball's color line with an urgent call for integration; he simply shifted responsibility to each individual team. Indeed, despite Smith's polling data, which suggested that at least a few Major League executives were open to integration, no team had pulled the trigger... at least not yet. But there was a man in a cluttered office in

Brooklyn—the same town where Effa's Eagles had played their first game—who was ready to change that.

Branch Rickey wasn't afraid to take calculated risks. He was an executive with a proven track record who had left the St. Louis Cardinals, a perennial powerhouse, to become the president and general manager of the lackluster Brooklyn Dodgers. He was a man of innovation and business intuition, and he was determined to help his new team prosper both during and after the war.

That meant finding the best players possible, no matter where they came from. Or what they looked like.

BEST-LAID PLANS

Branch Rickey initially joined the St. Louis Cardinals in 1919 as the organization's on-field manager. His baseball experience was vast: Rickey had played in college and the pros, including with the Major League St. Louis Browns; he also coached the University of Michigan's baseball team while attending law school there.

Unfortunately, Rickey's expertise failed to have a positive impact on the Cardinals' winning percentage. In 1925, tired of finishing no higher than third place in league standings, Cardinals owner Sam Breadon fired Rickey... but he didn't force him out of the organization completely.

Out of respect for Rickey's baseball knowledge and a hunch

Before becoming one of the most well-known executives in Major League Baseball history, Branch Rickey began his career in the Majors as a player with the St. Louis Browns of the American League.

that he might be better suited for the front office, Breadon moved the fledgling mogul to the position of general manager and tasked him with planning the Cardinals' overall business strategy. This transition would forever alter the trajectory of Rickey's career, for it was in that role—well before he led the charge for Major League Baseball's integration—that Rickey established himself as one of the game's foremost thinkers, someone who would one day be enshrined in the National Baseball Hall of Fame.

Under Rickey's front-office leadership, the Cardinals became a powerhouse club, winning their first World Series in 1926 and claiming the National League pennant in 1928 and 1930. The Cardinals secured additional National League titles in 1931, 1934, and 1942, while also being crowned World Series champions.

As with all winning teams, the Cardinals were doing lots of things right, but one major source of St. Louis's good fortune was undoubtedly its surplus of strong young talent, which Rickey cultivated through the team's first-of-its-kind farm system. The goal was to increase the team's profits as well as its ability to win games, and Rickey's player-development system did both.

With the help of scouts scattered throughout the country, Rickey signed unproven players at bargain prices and then trained them on minor-league teams within the organization. Then, when the players were ready for the big leagues, he simply called them up to play for the Cardinals. It was much cheaper than buying the contracts of already developed athletes from other teams, and once the players were no longer a good fit for the Cardinals, Rickey could earn an even greater profit by selling them on the open market.

Even as Commissioner Landis pushed back against Rickey's efforts—he believed the farm system would make minor-league baseball irrelevant—Rickey pressed forward, solidifying the precursor to today's minor-league system and maintaining a steady flow of well-trained players in the Cardinals organization. Meanwhile, competing teams that hadn't established their own talent pipelines were left scrambling for new blood to replace aging or injured players. This was certainly the case in Brooklyn, where Rickey landed in late 1942, after more than two decades with the Cardinals.

The Brooklyn Dodgers had won the pennant in 1941, but they were no match for the Cardinals in '42, thanks to a Rickey-recruited corps of players that included Hall of Famers Stan Musial and Enos Slaughter. The Dodgers' leadership was committed to building a winning club, however, and if anyone could help them do that, it was Rickey. The bespectacled executive, now in his sixties, took one look at the Brooklyn roster and made his assessment: The players were old and washed-up.

∗∗∗

According to Arthur Mann, Rickey's biographer and former assistant, the baseball boss may have been mulling over the idea of bringing Black players into the Majors as early as 1936. In a letter to Cardinals pitcher Dizzy Dean, Rickey chastised the star pitcher for stating that he would only play for the club if Bill DeLancey was his catcher. In his rebuke, he reminded Dean that he should be prepared to do his job no matter who was crouched behind home plate:

[Y]ou should write me an unqualified letter of assurance that you will be found this coming season with your shoulder to the wheel, supporting [Cardinals manager] Mr. Frisch from the beginning to the end of the baseball season, and that you will wear your uniform constantly in the ranks, good soldier, well-disciplined, pitching your head off when called upon regardless of who the catcher might be, black or white, young or old.

Rickey may have long considered the possibility of signing a Black player, but he also knew that gaining support for that decision wouldn't be easy. There was no need to broach the issue in St. Louis, where the Cardinals were already perennial winners. But in Brooklyn, Rickey was charged with building a new dynasty from scratch, even while many athletes in their prime were being deployed for war.

With that in mind, Rickey devised a six-step program that would pave the way for the first Black man to play in Major League Baseball since Moses Fleetwood Walker had been forced out six decades prior:

1. *The backing and sympathy of the Dodgers' directors and stockholders, whose investment and civic standing had to be considered and protected.*

2. *Picking a Negro who would be the right man on the field.*

3. *Picking a Negro who would be the right man off the field.*

4. *A good reaction from press and public.*

5. *Backing and thorough understanding from the Negro race, to avoid misrepresentation and abuse of the project.*

6. *Acceptance of the player by teammates.*

During a meeting with the Dodgers' board members in early 1943, Rickey carefully explained his plan for improving the team's fortunes. It would hinge on the mass recruitment of fresh talent. "That might include a Negro player or two," he added.

Rickey hesitated after speaking, unsure how his new bosses would respond. Discussion about Black athletes playing in the Majors had reached a fever pitch—both inside and outside the media—so Rickey knew the Dodgers' brass had at least thought about it. Still, he had no idea where they stood on the matter.

After a brief silence, George McLaughlin, the president of the Brooklyn Trust Company, which owned half of the Dodgers, put

Rickey at ease. "I don't see why not," he said. "You might come up with something. If you find the man who is better than the others, you'll beat it."

According to Murray Polner, another Rickey biographer, McLaughlin's response was considerably more pointed—and it put to rest any notion that his backing was motivated by anything other than the Dodgers' success: "If you're doing this to improve the ball club, go ahead. But if you're doing it for the emancipation of the Negro, then forget it."

Regardless of the intent behind the effort, improving the Dodgers ball club would be easier than ever; after all, Abe, Effa, and other Black team owners weren't just developing players, they were also sending out press releases and staging special events so the world could take notice. Because of their efforts, many of Black baseball's best players were no longer complete unknowns, hidden in the shadows of racism; they were out in the open where Rickey and others could find them.

As an added bonus, integrating the Majors was sure to boost the profits of any team daring enough to do it. Black fans loved baseball, and even though they'd long supported white teams, their love for their favorite Black players was unparalleled. Rickey knew that if he signed a talented Black player to join his team, the financial support from the Black community would be all but guaranteed.

After the meeting with the Dodgers' board members, Rickey could confidently cross off the first step of his plan.

Up next? Finding the perfect Black player.

***

While Black newspapers like the *Pittsburgh Courier, Chicago Defender,* and *Kansas City Call* had long been among Black baseball's most ardent supporters, reporters like the *Courier*'s Wendell Smith were never satisfied with covering the segregated teams of the Negro Leagues. They wanted to see the best Black players join the Majors, and they were developing their own plans to make it happen. Galvanized by Smith's integration poll and the relatively positive statement from Commissioner Landis, Smith and his colleagues began calling on their connections to arrange Major League tryouts for select Negro Leagues players.

On April 6, 1945, Jimmy Smith, sportswriter for the *Courier*'s Harlem bureau, and Joe Bostic, sports editor of the *People's Voice,* accompanied two Black players to the Brooklyn Dodgers' training camp at Bear Mountain, New York. With Dodgers manager Leo Durocher and Clyde Sukeforth, a coach and adviser to Rickey, looking on, pitcher Terris McDuffie of the Newark Eagles and out-fielder Dave "Showboat" Thomas of the New York Cubans tried their best to impress. But the resultant tryout was uneventful, and given the age of the players (thirty-five and forty, respectively), nothing came of it.

A week and a half later, Wendell Smith arranged an audition with the Boston Red Sox and chose Marvin Williams, second baseman for the Philadelphia Stars; Sam Jethroe, outfielder for the Cleveland Buckeyes; and Jackie Robinson, shortstop for the Kansas City Monarchs, to try out. Although Robinson was a rookie and had little experience in professional baseball, Smith knew his

Jackie Robinson (*right*) started his professional baseball career with the Kansas City Monarchs of the Negro American League, alongside pitching great Satchel Paige (*left*), before being signed to the Brooklyn Dodgers organization.

background would make him an ideal candidate for integration. In addition to being a four-sport star at UCLA, Robinson was an army veteran who'd spent plenty of time around white people.

When the men arrived at Fenway, Smith was surprised to see that Williams, Jethroe, and Robinson were the only Major League contenders at the park. The rest of the players were high schoolers who were clearly competing for entry-level positions in the Red Sox's farm system. Smith hadn't intended for the Black players to become minor-leaguers in white baseball, but after the manager and general manager of the Red Sox declined to speak to either Smith or the players he'd brought along, the sportswriter realized that the Negro Leaguers weren't even being considered for entry-level spots.

Like McDuffie and Thomas before them, Williams, Jethroe, and Robinson left the tryout without a Major League contract. But even though both auditions were unsuccessful, they were still proof that baseball's wall between Black and white was starting to crumble. This, Effa and the other owners could be sure of. What they didn't know was when the color line would be crossed—or what would happen to the Negro Leagues in the process.

✳✳✳

With integration looming, Effa's efforts to clean up Black baseball became more critical than ever. She continued to push for the timely reporting of game results to Black newspapers, the appointment of a neutral league commissioner, and a greater respect of Negro Leagues contracts from both owners and players. Though she fully supported the idea of Black players signing to Major League teams, Effa wasn't about to let Black baseball languish. Not when there had been so much time and money invested in the Negro Leagues. Not with the livelihoods of so many people resting on the futures of teams like the Newark Eagles, the Homestead Grays, and the Kansas City Monarchs.

"Let's be extremely careful from the beginning," Effa told a group of trade unionists, sportswriters, and public officials who had gathered to address the issue of Major League Baseball's color line in 1945. "I would like to see just one player break the ice, and he would have to be the finest player we have."

With the right player chosen, someone who could "meet the very toughest of big-league standards," Effa sensed that Major League Baseball would come back to recruit even more players— players who had been nurtured and developed by the Black owners and managers of the Negro National and Negro American Leagues.

Effa felt it would be in the best interest of the Negro Leagues, then, to form a partnership with Major League Baseball, to perhaps have Black teams become official farm clubs of the white ones. This plan would keep Black baseball in operation, and it would also support integration by providing a steady stream of Black talent for the Majors.

But Major League Baseball didn't get behind Effa's suggestions. Instead, it left the Negro Leagues to fend for themselves.

"After much shuttling back and forth I finally was granted an audience with the president of the national minor league organization," Effa wrote in her memoir. "He was quite courteous, and all that, but I could see that I was getting nowhere. And so the matter ended right then and there."

That wasn't actually the end of the matter, however. How Black players would be worked into Major League Baseball, and what would become of Black baseball overall, was still to be seen. In the interim, Effa had a team to run. And as the push toward integration continued to build momentum, she learned that her Eagles might soon face some additional competition from an unexpected source.

CROSSING THE LINE

Effa was sitting at her desk, handling the Eagles' early-season affairs, when the sound of her ringing phone jangled through the office.

"Mrs. Manley?" a voice said when Effa picked up. "This is Mr. Branch Rickey's secretary calling. Mr. Rickey would like to know if you would be available for a meeting in his office one day next week."

Effa's mind began swirling with questions. She could have never expected a call from Rickey's office, let alone an invitation to meet with him. It was May 1945, a full decade after the Manleys had first arranged for the Brooklyn-based Eagles to play home games at Ebbets Field. But despite the long-standing relationship with the ball club, Effa had yet to be personally introduced to the Dodgers' new leader.

It was a startling invitation, to say the least, and Effa just had to see what it was all about.

"Provided I am given enough notice," Effa told Rickey's secretary, "I could certainly make myself available."

✳✳✳

The following week, Effa walked into Branch Rickey's office for what she would later say was "one of the strangest conferences I have attended in all of my life."

There would be no one-on-one meeting with Rickey, no discussion of how they could possibly work together to address baseball's stubborn color line. No, as Effa looked around and counted more than thirty reporters—Black and white men representing nearly every newspaper in New York—she realized that Rickey was planning to make an announcement.

"I have decided to lend my support to a brand-new venture," Rickey said. "A new Negro organization, called the United States League, has been formed. I have called this press conference in order to clear up a lot of things."

Effa thought back to January, when news first broke that Pittsburgh Crawfords owner Gus Greenlee was starting a new Black baseball league, the same United States League that Rickey had just mentioned. It was no surprise that Greenlee wanted to get back into baseball; the wartime success of the Negro Leagues was largely due to his efforts in laying Black baseball's new foundation in the early 1930s, after all. But Effa couldn't understand why Rickey would get behind this new venture. Not only were both the Negro National and Negro American Leagues still in existence, but they had both been denying Greenlee's reentry for years.

After recovering from the financial difficulties that forced him out of the NNL in 1939, Greenlee tried to rejoin the league in 1941. He was denied that year and every year after; his attempts to join the NAL were rebuffed as well. As a result, Greenlee had been operating his Crawfords as an independent team, but no one knew more than him the benefits of an organized league structure.

While Effa tried to make sense of it all—the meeting, the new league, Rickey's intentions—the Dodgers president snatched a sheet of paper from atop one of the teetering piles on his desk and began to read from it.

First, he made clear there would be no mention of the

elephant-size topic on everyone's mind. "It is not my purpose to discuss today colored players becoming members of clubs in our present organized baseball leagues, or of white players becoming members of the proposed colored baseball league," he said.

Rickey also addressed the existing Black baseball leagues, but not in the way Effa had hoped. In fact, he claimed that the NNL and NAL didn't even qualify as professional leagues: "There are a number of colored teams, with more or less fixed identities, throughout the country, and none of these is a member of any league whatever in the sense of a 'league' in organized baseball," he said. "The United States League is now taking and will continue to take those first steps to bring about an effective organization."

Rickey then tossed out the names of the teams that would make up the new USL, including the Chicago Brown Bombers, the Toledo Rays, and Greenlee's Pittsburgh Crawfords. Also among the group was the Brooklyn Brown Dodgers, which Rickey promised would have full access to Ebbets Field when his Dodgers were out of town.

Effa glanced around at the reporters scribbling in their notebooks, their heads nodding in unison, as Rickey continued reading his statement.

He promised that the organization would be like nothing Negro baseball had ever seen, that it would be operated professionally and efficiently. He said that he would personally see to it that every attempt was made to have the United States League become a working member of organized baseball. And suddenly, with glaring clarity, Effa understood.

U. S. Negro League Is Launched With Brown Dodgers in Brooklyn

6-Club Circuit Announced at Ebbets Field Offices of Rickey—Hope Expressed for Recognition by Organized Ball

The formation of the United States Negro Baseball League was announced yesterday at a conference at Branch Rickey's Brooklyn club office. Rickey, except for his position as operator of Ebbets Field, where games will be played, and for his interest in the welfare of Negro baseball will not be connected with the organization.

Six teams form the new loop, with Brooklyn represented by the Brown Dodgers. Other members are Hilldale, Pa., Detroit, Chicago, Toledo and the Pittsburgh Crawfords. Major league parks contracted for are Ebbets Field, Wrigley Field, Chicago, and Forbes Field, Pittsburgh. Five home dates have been arranged for the Brooklyn nine, the first being set for May 24 against Hilldale.

No Major League Connection

At the beginning of the conference, attended by club-owners and writers, Rickey made it clear that "it is not my purpose to discuss today Negro players becoming members of clubs in our present organized baseball league or of white players becoming members of the proposed Negro baseball league."

Rickey said he hoped the league would become a model for all circuits to follow, that a sound structure would come out of it and that the league, in turn, would be accepted by the National Association of Professional Baseball Clubs. Such acceptance would make league players eligible to be drafted by the majors.

When this point was stressed, Rickey declined to enter into a discussion concerning the possibilities of Negro players eventually playing in the big leagues. He said he had made that clear in his opening remarks.

Hall to Operate Dodgers

The new league not to be confused with the Negro National or Negro American Leagues, which have been operating for the past ten years, will have as its president John Shackleford, Negro lawyer from Cleveland. A graduate of Wiley College and of the University of Michigan Law School, Shackleford also is a former independent ball player.

Rickey disclosed that he had leased Ebbets Field to Joe Hall, who will operate the Brown Dodgers. Following is the team's schedule for games at Ebbets Field:

May 24, Hilldale; 27, Pittsburgh Crawfords; June 6, Hilldale (night game); 12, Chicago.

Branch Rickey's 1945 announcement about the development of the new United States League concerned Effa, as she wondered why he didn't support the Negro Leagues that were already in existence.

"Organized baseball" was code for Major League Baseball, for the white teams that had not only shut out Black players but had also been less than accommodating to Effa and the other Negro Leagues owners who had tried to form an alliance with them. Rickey clearly had plans for the integration of the Majors, but those plans did not include Effa or the other owners of NNL and NAL teams.

Finally, Rickey opened the floor to questions, and with anger and betrayal rising in her chest, Effa jumped right in. "This thing is hitting us very suddenly right between the eyes," she said before adding, "Mr. Rickey, if you are so interested in Negro baseball, as all this would lead us to believe, then why in the world didn't you contact our two present Negro Leagues so that we might try to work out all this on a mutual basis?"

The heads of the reporters jerked upright, like puppets on a string. Rickey, not the least bit flustered, responded quickly. "Good question, Mrs. Manley. I'm glad you asked. Attorney Shackleford, would you please answer Mrs. Manley?"

Effa's eyes followed Rickey's to a Black man who had been identified as the president of the new league. "Mrs. Manley, we did write letters to the presidents of both of your leagues," Shackleford said. "[Negro American League] President Martin wrote back that he wasn't at all interested in our proposition. [Negro National League] President Wilson hasn't answered us to this day."

"Does that answer your question?" Rickey said, turning back to Effa.

Effa hesitated. "Well, it's a very confusing kind of answer. I don't know just what to say to all of this."

＊＊＊

After Rickey's press conference, Effa rushed back to her office to fill the other NNL owners in on his plans. She still wasn't sure about

Rickey's motives, but she was definitely worried that the United States League would present a level of competition that the NNL couldn't withstand. Effa soon discovered, however, that the other owners didn't share her concern.

The USL would struggle, they surmised, because the new teams wouldn't be able to schedule games in many of the Major League parks. Rickey had promised access to all the stadiums owned by the Dodgers organization, but that couldn't account for all the other league games that would need to be played in order for the USL to make enough money to stay in business. The NNL owners had cultivated relationships with the New York Yankees, Washington Senators, and other teams over many years, and a new league—even one supported by Branch Rickey—wouldn't be able to encroach upon that occupied territory.

In the end, Effa's colleagues were correct that the United States League would struggle to compete with the more established NNL. Still, their responses revealed a naivete about Rickey's ability to upend the operations of their own teams. By the time the USL folded in 1946, hampered by a lack of stadium access as well as top talent, Branch Rickey's six-step plan to integrate baseball was nearly complete.

Shortly after announcing his involvement with the United States League, Rickey had a conversation with the *Pittsburgh Courier's* Wendell Smith. He'd compiled a list of well-known Black players, including Satchel Paige, Josh Gibson, and others, but he wasn't sure that any of them were the ideal choice to cross Major League Baseball's color line. He wanted Smith's take, to see if maybe he had overlooked a player or two.

When Smith told Rickey about Jackie Robinson, whom he'd taken to the Red Sox tryout, the Brooklyn mogul was filled with intrigue. "Jackie Robinson!" he exclaimed. "I knew he was an All-American football player and an All-American basketball player, but I didn't know he played baseball."

Rickey promised that Smith would hear from him soon and went to work investigating the former UCLA star; in August, he sent scout Clyde Sukeforth to Chicago to see Robinson in action with the Monarchs. There was some question about the strength of Robinson's arm, but Rickey gave Sukeforth the authority to make the final call on the shortstop's potential. "If you like his arm, Clyde, and if his schedule will permit, bring him in," Rickey said. "Get him away from his teammates so that nobody will know what you're talking about. I want absolute secrecy."

Over many months before Jackie Robinson became the first Black player to sign a contract with a Major League team in more than sixty years, Brooklyn Dodgers scouts traveled to see Robinson play and determine whether he had the skills to make it in the Majors.

At the end of the month, on August 28, 1945, Robinson did meet Rickey in his office—the same office where Effa had listened to Rickey promise to bring professionalism, efficiency, and integrity to the Negro Leagues. But when he met with Robinson during those last days of summer, as another baseball season was coming to an end, Rickey's focus wasn't on a new Black team or league.

It was on one specific Black player...a player who, with his help, would change the course of baseball, and American history, forever.

***

Meanwhile, as Rickey was continuing his clandestine recruitment of Robinson and others, Effa was working to ensure that Black teams, coaches, and executives—not just Black players—had a future in professional baseball. Despite the criticism they'd received, Effa knew the Negro Leagues were a respectable enterprise with professional teams and top-tier talent. She was so sure of this, in fact, that she was willing to prove it.

Effa had the chance to do just that in October 1945, after she received another invitation from the Brooklyn Dodgers. This time, the club wanted to know if she could put together an All-Star team of Black players to face off against a team of white All-Stars in a double-header at Ebbets Field. Presumably, Rickey wanted to use the exhibition to get a good look at the best Black ballplayers, and to see how they handled themselves against white competition.

Despite the rigid color line in Major League Baseball, play between Black and white teams still occurred regularly in the sport, and those integrated games were often some of the most profitable on the schedule for Black clubs. Most often, the white teams facing off against all-Black teams were semipro outfits, but the exhibition proposed by the Dodgers was a much bigger event. It was an opportunity for Effa to garner long-overdue respect for the Negro Leagues. If Branch Rickey was forced to acknowledge the color-blind greatness of Black players, Effa believed he would also have to acknowledge the organizations that nurtured and developed them.

To make the competition an even bigger event, Effa persuaded the Dodgers to extend the series to five games. She then went to work recruiting the best Black talent available, a task that became all the more critical once she received a verbal challenge from Dodgers third-base coach Charlie Dressen, who would manage the white team.

"I have the best All-Star team ever assembled," Dressen said. "Get your best Negroes to meet us. Get Satchel Paige, get Gibson—"

"Wait a minute," Effa said, refusing to be intimidated. "I'll get the best there are, if your team is really that good, but you let me pick 'em . . . If we can win

Sept. 29 1945

Dear Sam;

I just received some publicity and pictures from Brooklyn, and decided to send this one to you to see if there was a chance to get it in the paper this week. I will of course take an add as usual.

Green has promised to get together with us Sunday night at The Thresa, and I am almost sure he will try and help us to get a good team together. As things stand now, it looks like Pearson at 1st (his arm is alright), Bankhead at 2nd, Austin in short, and Watkins at 3rd. Irvin, Davis, and Harvey in the outfield, Newcombe, Hooker, Partlow, and we are going to try to get Byrd, and Campenello from Green.

If I had known there were going to be so many games played after Sept. I might have hesitated a little before going ahead. When I received the first call asking about getting a team together, I got in touch with Satchell, and asked him would he take part. He said he would, but they eveidently arranged his tour after that. There is more behind it but I will tell you when I see you. I dont want to write everything.

The games should be a big attraction, but of course my big concern is having our boys look good. It will give us a chance to make Larry McPhail look bad, if we can look good. I wish it was possible to have Josh, Satchell, and Wellmaker, maybe even Benjamin, but I guess we will be alright. If you have any suggestion to make please get in touch with me. I know you are as anxious to have the Negro's come through as I am.

Just before the much-anticipated five-game series between Effa's Negro League All-Stars and the team of white All-Stars led by Dodgers coach Chuck Dressen, Effa wrote to sportswriter Sam Lacy about the matchup. Her biggest concern: "having our boys look good."

this series, it will do more to advance the cause of Negroes in the Major Leagues than half a dozen of these conferences we have been having."

Staying true to her word, Effa tried to secure Paige for the series and even offered him $1,000 to pitch. Paige was heading out on his own barnstorming tour, though, and was unable to commit, but Effa did add Roy Campanella, catcher for the Baltimore Elite Giants; Frank Austin, shortstop for the Philadelphia Stars; and Johnny Wright, a right-handed pitcher for the Homestead Grays, to the lineup. They joined Eagles standouts (and future Hall of Famers) Monte Irvin, an outfielder who hit for power and average, and Don Newcombe, an up-and-coming hurler who would go on to win the Cy Young Award, the honor given to Major League Baseball's most dominant pitcher in a season.

The series was destined to be a battle for the ages—on paper, at least.

"If my boys hit the ball out of Ebbets Field against [Dodgers pitchers Ralph] Branca and [Hal] Gregg, and if my boys hold your sluggers in check, how are the big league magnates going to answer to us?" Effa asked Dressen.

"I have some hitters, too," he replied. "Imagine a ball club on which Frank McCormick of the Reds [who had been se-lected to eight straight National League All-Star teams] will have to hit six! Up ahead of him will be [Dodger Eddie] Stanky, [Dodger Goody] Rosen, [Pittsburgh Pirate Johnny] Barrett, [St. Louis Cardinal Whitey] Kurowski and [Pirate] Jimmy Russell. The power alone would have won the National League pennant by ten games!"

✳✳✳

The much-hyped exhibition got off to a dramatic start on the rain-soaked afternoon of Sunday, October 7.

In the first game of the doubleheader, Dressen's team came out hard and fast, scoring one run in the bottom of the first in-ning and another in the third. When Effa's team answered with one run in the top of the fourth and three runs in the top of the seventh, the Black All-Stars were finally on top. The lead, however, was short-lived. The white All-Stars scored two more runs in the bottom of the eighth, locking the score at 4–all going into the last frame.

In the top of the ninth, Effa's team was unable to capitalize on their last chance at the plate; at that point, all they could do was hope to shut out Dressen's squad in the bottom of the inning. But with two out and a runner on third, the Black All-Stars' dreams were dashed. Stanky hit a single that scored the winning run for the white team.

Play was similarly close in Game 2. Dressen's team scored a run in the bottom of the second inning to go up 1–0. Effa's team scored its first run in the top of the fourth to tie the game, but a triple by Jimmy Russell in the bottom of the fourth, followed by a passed ball, brought home the go-ahead run for the white team. Unfortunately for the Black All-Stars, the one-run differential would remain. The game was called because of darkness after five innings with the score frozen at 2–1 in favor of the Dressen All-Stars.

After four days of rest, the two teams met for a rematch in Newark on Friday, October 12. Effa hoped the time off would invigorate her squad, but the results were the same—albeit far more convincing. The Major Leaguers shut out the Negro Leaguers and ran away to a 10–0 victory in Game 3 of the series.

Heading into the weekend, Effa's team had only two more chances to redeem itself—yet the first attempt was quickly squandered.

Back at Ebbets Field on Sunday, October 14, in front of a crowd of about ten thousand enraptured fans, Detroit Tigers pitcher Virgil Trucks proved himself the hero of Game 4. Besides holding the Black All-Stars to just four hits and one run, Trucks smashed a double off the right-field wall in the bottom of the eighth that allowed one of his teammates to score. He also scored the white team's fourth and final run when he was driven home by a Barrett single in the same inning. Final score: 4–1, Dressen All-Stars.

With only one game left in the series, Dressen's team had notched four wins. Effa's team had none. She was demoralized, certainly... But she was also hopeful.

Game 5 proved to be a pitchers' duel, with Black hurler Johnny Wright clearly dominant. He gave up just three hits through five innings, holding the Dressen All-Stars scoreless. Finally, it seemed, the Black All-Stars would be able to overtake their white counterparts. But there was one major problem: Effa's team was scoreless, too. When that game was called, the score was still 0–0, and the Black team had failed to win even one game against the white All-Stars.

Under the headline, DRESSEN'S CLUB TOO POWERFUL, the *Brooklyn Daily Eagle* drew the only obvious conclusion from the All-Star series results: "For the present, Major League baseball as played in the National and American League is superior to that of the Negro National League."

Effa disagreed with such a sweeping generalization, but she couldn't deny that her players' performance had been subpar. In a letter to Vernon Green, vice president of the Baltimore Elite Giants, Effa expressed her frustration about costly errors, noted that the Black All-Stars should have won the first game in Brooklyn, and conceded that if the absolute best Black players—including Paige and Gibson—had been available, the outcome of the series would have likely been different. "I think a lot of it was stage fright," she added, "but I really got the impression also that they just did not know what to do half the time."

The loss to the Major Leaguers may have devastated Effa, but it was ultimately of little consequence. Rickey's integration gears were already in motion.

Rickey openly recruited catcher Roy Campanella during the series, though Campy, like the rest of the sports world, thought Rickey was only interested in Black players for his Brown Dodgers team. Rickey also got a good look at Johnny Wright, the pitcher who kept the Dressen All-Stars scoreless in Game 5. Most significantly, though the public didn't know it at the time, Rickey had already secured Jackie Robinson's playing services for the Brooklyn Dodgers organization: The following season, Robinson was to join the Montreal Royals, one of the Dodgers' minor-league affiliates.

The formal announcement of Jackie Robinson's signing was made on October 23, 1945, and newspapers across the country lauded the move as a victory for all of Black America. Effa, meanwhile, wasn't so sure.

Just a week after her all-Black lineup had failed to hold its own against top white players, Effa had even more reason to wonder whether Black baseball would be washed away in the wave of integration. "Robinson is the property of the Kansas City Monarchs," she said when questioned by the *Brooklyn Daily Eagle*. "Until I know his status in the matter, I will have to remain silent."

THE THIEF OF NEW YORK

Effa was right to be worried about the future of Black baseball. When the initial noise around Jackie Robinson's signing began to die down, Effa and the other Negro Leagues team owners were horrified to learn that Rickey, under the guise of "progress," had stolen Robinson away from the Monarchs.

Just like modern sports teams, Negro Leagues clubs invested a lot of money in the development of their players, and every player contract carried its own value —a value based, primarily, on the athlete's skills and ability to draw a crowd. The contract of a once-in-a-lifetime talent like Satchel Paige was certainly worth more than that of a run-of-the-mill rookie, but every contract was worth *something*.

If a team wanted to recruit any player from another ball club, that team was required to compensate the player's current club based on the value of the player's contract. There were often trades wherein one team would exchange a player of equal value for the player they wanted to acquire. However, when Rickey recruited Robinson, he could not trade a white Dodgers player to the all-Black Kansas City Monarchs. The only other option, then, was for Rickey to make a cash payment to the Monarchs—to buy Robinson's contract.

Rickey knew this, of course. He was well versed in the financial realities of running a baseball team and understood the monetary significance of baseball players. In fact, while in St. Louis, Rickey routinely sold player contracts to other teams in order to bring in cash that could offset dips in ticket sales, the huge expense of the Cardinals' minor-league system, or any other financial setbacks. Rickey once estimated that, during his twenty-five-year tenure with the Cardinals, he'd earned the club between $2.5 million and $3 million this way.

But despite his own business savvy—or maybe because of it—Rickey never compensated the Monarchs for Robinson's contract, nor did he even reach out to Monarchs owners Tom Baird and J. L. Wilkinson to discuss a potential deal.

While Branch Rickey's 1945 signing of Jackie Robinson was hailed as racial progress, the future of the Negro Leagues was still uncertain.

In his biography of his former boss, Arthur Mann asserts that, during their very first meeting, Rickey asked Robinson about his contractual obligations. According to Mann, Robinson said that he had neither an oral or written agreement stipulating how long he was to play for the Monarchs; he told Rickey that he simply worked "from payday to payday."

Despite the corroboration of other details about the meeting, Robinson doesn't mention this particular exchange in his own autobiography, *I Never Had It Made*. But given Rickey's considerable experience handling player contracts, his conversation with Robinson stands out. If he had been recruiting a white player from a white team, any potential trade would have been discussed owner to owner, not directly with the player in a covert meeting.

Indeed, when Monarchs owner Baird protested Rickey's handling of Robinson's signing, Rickey made his opinions of Black baseball and its contracts clear once again. "The Negro organizations in baseball are not leagues, nor, in my opinion, do they have an organization," he declared.

In the end, there was little the Monarchs owners could do in response to Rickey's pilfering ways. When pressed, Baird acknowledged that he didn't *technically* have a signed contract with Robinson. They'd come to an agreement via telegrams and letters, Baird said, and he believed that their correspondence was as binding as a contract. Rickey, on the other hand, thought it proved his point about the shoddy structure of Black baseball.

Despite the lack of a formal agreement between Robinson and the Monarchs, there was still the possibility that a judge would have ruled in Baird and Wilkinson's favor if they had chosen to take Rickey and the Dodgers to court. Realistically, though, filing suit was a lose-lose proposition. Aside from the tremendous cost, the Monarchs couldn't afford to anger the Black community by appearing to stand in the way of Robinson's future in white baseball.

As Effa and the owners discovered, Black baseball fans were unequivocal supporters of integration, and they gave little thought to the business of baseball. They didn't consider that player contracts were tangible assets no different from cases of baseballs or a closet full of uniforms, and that if another team wanted to recruit an already-signed player, his contract had to be purchased at a fair price. Thus, they didn't understand that Rickey's poaching of Robinson amounted to thievery, nor did they contemplate what would happen to the Negro Leagues once other Black players were lured away from their teams.

As Clark Griffith, owner of the Washington Senators, spoke out in support of the Negro Leagues, many called attention to his conflict of interest. Like other owners of white baseball teams, Griffith made a significant amount of money from renting his stadiums to Black baseball teams each year.

While most of Rickey's colleagues in Major League Baseball remained silent on the matter, Clark Griffith, owner of the Washington Senators, was one of the few white executives who spoke out against Rickey's actions.

"While it is true that we have no agreement with Negro Leagues—National and American—we still can't act like outlaws in taking their stars," Griffith said. "We have no right to destroy them. There is such a thing as an unwritten law in such cases. In no walk of life can one person take another's property unless he pays for it. If Brooklyn wants to buy Robinson from Kansas City, that would be all right, but contracts of Negro teams should be recognized by organized baseball."

Not surprisingly, Griffith's takedown elicited an equally pointed response from Rickey: "Clark Griffith, to the contrary, I have not signed a player from what I regard as an organized league."

Rickey also claimed that, in his estimated three years of scouting Black players, he'd never found one with a contract.

"Of course they [have contracts]," Griffith snapped, "and they suspend and fine players the same as we do."

On its surface, Griffith's defense of Black baseball seemed laudable. But to some members of the Black community, his critique of Rickey was high on performance and short on sincerity.

Several months earlier, on May 26, 1945, Wendell Smith had taken to his *Courier* column to compare Rickey's and Griffith's support of the Negro Leagues. Rickey had just announced his involvement in the United States League, and Griffith, who earned a significant portion of his team's revenue by renting his stadium to Black teams, claimed to be wary of Rickey's intent. Smith had his own thoughts.

> No one seems to know why Rickey has taken such a sudden interest in the operations [of] Negro baseball... Whatever his motive, Rickey has advanced some good ideas and they are perfectly logical... Consequently, he certainly deserves the benefit of the doubt.

> On the other hand, Clark Griffith is one of the most bitter opponents of the forces advocating the admission of Negro players in the Major Leagues... Griffith is one of the big league owners who prefers to go outside the borders of these United States and bring in players, rather than hire American citizens of color. He goes thousands upon thousands of miles in quest of players, when he could sign up a Negro player in ten minutes. All he has to do is to look out the window of his office at Griffith Stadium on any day the Homestead Grays are playing there and see plenty of players good enough to play with the Senators.

Clark Griffith's defense of the present Negro leagues [over Rickey's newly formed United States League] is not motivated by anything but his own selfish interests. He makes money by renting his park to the Homestead Grays. He doesn't want any one fooling around with that profitable mellon [sic]. He'll do anything he can to help perpetuate the present setup in Negro baseball because it's to his advantage.

To be sure, Smith was completely justified in pointing out Griffith's biases. After all, the Senators' owner had a major financial stake in the sustained future of Black baseball. But in the process of discrediting Griffith and declaring the Senators' owner a racist prosegregationist, Smith inevitably put his faith in a man who may have been willing to sign a handful of Black players but who, ultimately, had no respect for Negro Leagues Baseball, or the men and women who'd built it.

* * *

As integration landed on baseball's doorstep ahead of the 1946 season, gathering a consensus on the right way to merge the worlds of white and Black baseball was proving impossible. Like Griffith,

Effa believed that Negro Leagues contracts should be respected and that owners of Black teams should be compensated for their players. She also believed that the Negro Leagues should be formally integrated into Major League Baseball as an official minor-league partner, but none of the white baseball executives, including Griffith, were advocating for that.

As it stood, the lens of integration became focused on opportunities for individual Black players, not for entire Black teams or leagues. And within the broader Black community, seeing those players join the rosters of white teams in Major League Baseball was the ultimate, best goal. For many in the Black community, the Negro Leagues had passed the point of usefulness. All-Black teams and leagues were previously necessary but no longer ideal, not when the Majors had finally eased open the door that had been bolted shut for so long. Whether Black players should actually walk through that door was never questioned; neither did anyone consider what lay on the other side. The fact that the door opened at all was the unquestionable proof of progress.

Nowhere was this more evident than in Jackie Robinson's journey from Negro Leagues rookie to Major League barrier-breaker. The signing of his Dodgers contract was a historic moment, certainly, but it was also one that was fraught with tension, a sign of tortuous things to come.

Years after joining the Dodgers organization, Robinson recounted his first meeting with his future employer, detailing how Rickey lashed him with degrading insults and described, in horrific detail, the abuse that Robinson was likely to face on the baseball field:

> *Suppose I was at shortstop. Another player comes down from first, stealing, flying in with spikes high, and cuts me on the leg. As I feel the blood running down my leg, the white player laughs in my face.*

> *"How do you like that, n———r boy?" he sneers.*

> *Could I turn the other cheek? I didn't know how I would do it. Yet I knew that I must.*

Rickey used this exercise to make his expectations clear: Robinson was to be a model player *and* man, someone who could simply absorb all the criticisms and indignities that were sure to be hurled at him. Not only was Robinson forbidden from retaliating, but he would have to smile when he wanted to cry and apologize when he'd done nothing wrong. Through it all, Robinson was to remain grateful for his marvelous blessing while ignoring its accompanying curses.

And he had to be perfect. Man, did he have to be perfect. There could be no missteps or wavering, as Robinson's signing would be the country's first experiment with integration that had national implications. This was not a light-skinned, middle-class Black woman in New York being hired alongside white women in a department store that had a predominantly Black customer base. This was a man with deep brown skin joining a team with white men who, in most cases, had never had a conversation with a Black person, let alone a relationship. Yet they would be thrust together to train and play and live. And they would have to travel to cities that were far less open to racial equality, where fans would be just as likely to show up to root *against* Robinson as they would be to cheer *for* their home team.

Indeed, as the 1940s gave way to the fifties and sixties, racial integration in America typically followed a similar pattern, regardless of industry: After proving themselves sufficiently worthy, a few Black people were hand-selected, ripped away from the safety and security of their communities, and allowed to enter all-white spaces. Once there, they ran straight into people who resented their presence and often retaliated with violence.

Yet there was never any sacrifice required of white people, no demand that they, too, step outside their comfort zones in the name of advancement. Even as their glass houses were shattered by the arrival of those whom they'd fought valiantly to keep out, whites still maintained the upper hand. Black people were sent crawling in through the back door, careful to not make a fuss. They were to be seen and not heard, lest they be booted right back into the street.

This was the standard to which Robinson had to adhere. It was what Branch Rickey demanded of him, but it was what all of white America would require as well.

**

Jackie Robinson was expected to turn the other cheek on the baseball diamond, and Black baseball executives were supposed to do the same behind the closed doors of their team offices. But as integration threatened to bankrupt their businesses, Effa and some of the other owners refused to remain silent.

In early November 1945, Effa helped Cum Posey, owner of the Homestead Grays and secretary of the Negro National League, write a letter to Major League Baseball's new commissioner, Happy Chandler. Though Effa never held an official title within the NNL, Posey and the other men recognized her value and often relied on her expertise, and she was eager to lend a hand to this matter in particular. The tiff between Effa and Posey of years prior had long been brushed aside; the only thing that mattered in the moment was the preservation of Black baseball.

Writing on behalf of both the Negro National and Negro American Leagues, Posey condemned the way Rickey had gone after Robinson and was continuing to poach Black players. Aside from his refusal to compensate Negro Leagues teams for the contracts of their players, Rickey was bypassing team executives to speak directly with the players about joining his team—a policy that was unheard of in both Black and white baseball.

"We feel that the clubs of Organized Negro Baseball who have gone to so much expense to develop players and establish teams and leagues should be approached and deals made between clubs involved even though Negro Organized Baseball is not a part of white Organized Baseball," Posey wrote. "That is the only way in which we can be assured that Negro Organized Baseball can continue to operate."

To close the letter, Posey invited Chandler to a Negro National League meeting that was scheduled for November 9, 1945, in New York City.

With that, Effa, Posey, and the other owners could only wait. And hope.

They hoped that Chandler would accept the invitation to the league meeting and, most important, they hoped that he would sympathize with the owners of Black baseball teams.

Meanwhile, as they awaited the commissioner's response, a letter of support from Washington Senators owner Clark Griffith imbued them with faith.

Your two Leagues have established a splendid reputation and now have the support and respect of the colored people all over the country as well as the decent white people. They have not pirated against organized baseball nor have they stolen anything from them and Organized Baseball has no moral right to take anything away from them without their consent…

I understand that Mr. Rickey told Commissioner Chandler that Robinson was not under contract to the Kansas City Club but whether he was or wasn't, he certainly made a verbal agreement with the Kansas City Club that he would play ball with them for so much per month. This in itself constitutes a contract, for, had Kansas City failed to pay him he could have gone to court and collected his salary.

Mr. Posey, anything that is worthwhile is worth fighting for, so you folks should leave not a stone unturned to protect the existence of your two established Negro Leagues. Don't let anybody tear it down…It is my belief that Commissioner will give you relief."

THE NEGRO
(LEAGUES) PROBLEM

Major League Baseball commissioner Happy Chandler did not attend the Negro Leagues owners' meeting on November 9. But on January 17, 1946, he and the presidents of the two Major Leagues met with representatives from the Negro American and Negro National Leagues in Cincinnati, Ohio.

It was the meeting Effa had hoped for, though she was unable to secure her own seat at the table. Instead, J. B. Martin, owner of the Chicago American Giants and NAL president, and Tom Wilson, owner of the Baltimore Elite Giants and NNL president, would be present to voice Black baseball's concerns about compensation for player contracts. At the same time, they hoped to advocate for a more equitable path toward baseball's integration.

Chandler, still early in his tenure as baseball's top boss after the 1944 death of Kenesaw Mountain Landis, was working on a plan to bring the white minor-league system under the same umbrella as the Majors. The plan had met some early resistance, though, with one league official noting, "They have their own organization and are happy with it."

Black baseball owners had their own organization, too, but whether they were "happy with it" was irrelevant. Integration was

After Kenesaw Mountain Landis's death in 1944, Happy Chandler (*pictured*) replaced him as the new commissioner of Major League Baseball and oversaw the tumultuous days of integration.

happening, and the Negro Leagues couldn't afford to remain independent—not if they hoped to stay in business or to be treated fairly in negotiations for their Black players.

So on that chilly January day, when Chandler offered the two most prominent Negro Leagues an opportunity similar to the one he'd offered the white minor leagues, the representatives from Black baseball jumped at the chance.

But first, before anything could become official, the owners would have to meet Chandler's stipulations.

"I told them to get their house in order, then come to baseball with a petition for recognition," Chandler announced during a January 21 press conference in Dallas, Texas. "I see no reason why the Negro Leagues cannot become a part of organized baseball with the commissioner serving them as he does other leagues."

Chandler's new guidelines for Black baseball were simple but not necessarily easy:

- Adopt a constitution similar to the one that governed Major League Baseball.
- Implement ironclad player contracts that would

prevent contract jumping as well as raids from other teams, similar to the ones used in the Majors.

- Build their own stadiums to decrease the power of third-party booking agents and the fees being paid to them.

Encouraged, the owners returned to their hometowns ready to implement Chandler's directives. Effa had been begging the other owners to improve their operations for years, and while it would have been best for them to take heed of her advice before Branch Rickey began plundering Black baseball teams and exposing all their flaws, if it took Rickey's brashness to finally inspire action, Effa wasn't going to complain.

The owners had already approved a new constitution and had formalized their player contracts. The issue of building stadiums, however, was more difficult to address. The increased profits of the war and postwar years still weren't enough to finance a stadium while meeting day-to-day expenses, and even the most financially secure Black owners had a much harder time obtaining bank loans than the average white entrepreneur. On top of all that, even if funding were not an issue, it would have taken months, if not years, to get a stadium's construction approved and completed—time they didn't have if they wanted to take advantage of Chandler's offer.

The owners had no choice but to abandon the prospect of building new stadiums, but with the new season approaching, they hoped that the efforts they had made would be enough to convince Chandler to follow through on his word.

Meanwhile, back in Brooklyn, Branch Rickey and the Dodgers were continuing their steady march toward integration.

✳ ✳ ✳

On January 29, Branch Rickey announced that he'd signed pitcher Johnny Wright, the right-handed ace who'd stunned against the Dressen All-Stars and was most recently a member of the Homestead Grays. Like Jackie Robinson, Wright was to begin his career with the minor-league Montreal Royals. And like Jackie Robinson, Wright had been whisked away from Black baseball without any consideration of a preexisting contract. While the hurler claimed that he was a free agent, Posey felt otherwise.

"We do not think this is a fair way of doing business," Cum Posey said of Rickey's continued raids. "We have no intention of standing in [Wright's] way of getting into organized baseball, but we feel that if he is good enough for the Dodgers' organization, they should be as willing to pay us for him as they would be to pay Milwaukee or St. Paul or Columbus for him if he were a white player."

But Rickey didn't stop with Robinson and Wright. In early April, Rickey also signed Roy Campanella, a catcher for the Baltimore Elite Giants, and Don Newcombe, a nineteen-year-old pitcher who had stumbled into Effa's office looking for his first pro contract just two years prior.

Effa understood Rickey's interest in Newcombe. The Dodgers president was a master at player development, and even though Newcombe had yet to become the MVP and Cy Young

In the seven months after Branch Rickey signed Jackie Robinson to the Brooklyn Dodgers organization, he signed four more Black players, including Roy Campanella (*left*) and Effa's own Don Newcombe (*right*).

Award–winning pitcher that he would in Brooklyn, he had promise and a blazing fastball. Still, understanding Rickey's actions and accepting them were two different things. Effa had long been upset about Rickey's tactics, but now he'd shown up in her own backyard.

Like Baird and Wilkinson of the Monarchs, Posey of the Grays, and Tom Wilson of the Elite Giants, Effa decided not to seek legal action against Rickey. Instead, her attorney advised her to write the Dodgers' president directly and request a meeting to discuss Newcombe's signing.

She did, but Rickey never responded.

"I think we look very stupid to sit tight and not open our mouth with the stuff he is pulling," Effa wrote in a letter to Seward Posey, Cum's brother and business manager of the Grays.

But what could they do? Commissioner Chandler refused to get involved in the issue of player compensation, so the relief that Clark Griffith believed would come never materialized. No one could stop Rickey, it seemed. In fact, no one could even question him.

Rickey's signings of Wright, Campanella, and Newcombe proved that his desire to bring Black players into the Majors was more than a gimmick. And because he was the first white executive willing to follow through on integration, Rickey earned the unconditional support of the Black community, especially as Black people became less and less interested in supporting segregated institutions.

At the *Pittsburgh Courier*, which had become one of the most widely read Black newspapers in the country, sportswriter Wendell Smith regularly leveraged his considerable influence to speak out about the erasure of baseball's color line. He was often critical of the Negro Leagues in the process, but his January 26, 1946, column was especially biting.

Not only did Smith decide that Black baseball leagues were no longer in the best interest of the Black community, but he also criticized the intentions of Negro Leagues executives who were unhappy with Rickey's efforts:

Anyone under the impression that the signing of Jackie Robinson was received with joyous acclaim within the portals of Negro baseball is sadly mistaken. While approximately 13 million Negroes and possibly a like number of whites received the announcement with enthusiasm, there was a sullen reaction and a frantic scramble to "save everything before the avalanche" inside the house of Negro baseball. So they went whimpering to Chandler, pleading for recognition and no further repetition of the "Robinson case." All they saw was the glittering gold they've been reaping for the past four years; all they envisioned was the crumbling of their bawdy house; all they cared about was the perpetuation of the "slave trade" they had developed via the channels of segregated baseball.

Smith's words left Effa feeling dejected and disappointed. The Negro Leagues owners had been cast aside by white organized baseball; now they were being ostracized by the very community they sought to serve. In his column, Smith hadn't mentioned how the owners had completely supported Robinson and the other Black players who'd recently signed contracts with white organized baseball, nor did he praise them for forgoing legal action against Rickey. He certainly didn't acknowledge all the work Effa and the other owners had done to try to bring the Majors and the Negro Leagues together in ways that would preserve autonomy and power for Black teams. In his column, Smith only attacked and accused.

But even with her spirits low and the probability of failure high, Effa was determined to keep fighting. Effa pledged to keep fighting for all of Black baseball, and with the 1946 Negro National League season just months away, she also fought to field the best Newark team ever.

With or without Newcombe, Effa's Eagles were going to win—and they were going to win *big*.

FLYING HIGH

While World War II represented a time of unparalleled prosperity for the Negro Leagues, it also took as much as it gave. On the Newark Eagles alone, pitchers Max Manning and Leon Day and second baseman Larry Doby were all drafted into the service. Effa was able to adjust and fill in the gaps of their absence, working overtime to develop the less experienced players on her roster, but she was delighted when they were able to rejoin the team in time for the 1946 season.

Manning, Day, and Doby came home to a roster brimming with talent, including a home run–hitting utility player from nearby Orange, New Jersey, named Monte Irvin. Irvin joined the Eagles in

1937, while still in high school, and he'd been a consistent presence ever since: His bat was strong, his legs quick, his heart loyal.

Like other Black players, Irvin received numerous offers to play in Latin America in the spring and summer months, but he always kept his commitment to Effa and the Eagles. At least he always did until 1942, when he received an offer he couldn't refuse.

Just a few days after the Eagles' 1942 home opener, Irvin received a letter from Jorge Pasquel, a Mexican businessman and owner of the Mexican League's Azules de Veracruz team. Pasquel wanted Irvin to join his club for the remainder of the '42 season, and he was willing to pay him a considerable amount of money to do so.

Before he made a decision, Irvin told Effa about the offer. He also said that if she gave him a raise of $25 per month, he would stay in Newark.

"Monte, you're young," Effa told him. "You got plenty of time to make your fortune."

But Irvin wasn't trying to make a fortune. In fact, he'd always been grateful for his baseball salary. When he first joined the team at a rate of $125 per month, he knew it was far more than what most Black men were making at the time; his own father had never earned more than half that.

Five years had passed, though, and Irvin understood that his value as a player had increased. He was also planning to marry his high school sweetheart and start a family, so he needed the extra cash.

"Jorge wants to give me five hundred a month plus two hundred for an apartment plus a maid," Irvin told Effa. "But I want to play on this team. It's the best team I've ever been on. We'll fill the park, make a great reputation for ourselves."

Effa wavered, but only slightly. It had been just a few months since she and Abe had considered leaving the Negro National League after the resounding defeat of Judge Rainey, their nominee for league president. In a letter to sportswriter Art Carter, Effa explained that Abe was the reason they decided to stick around, that he wanted to see if he could make back any of the money he'd invested in the Eagles over the years. "If it had been left to me we would be through," she added.

Given their precarious financial circumstances, Effa continued to hold the Eagles' purse strings tight. And because she was unwilling to dip into her till to pay Irvin any more money, he left.

Irvin played in Mexico in 1942 and was drafted into the army once the season ended. After a few years fighting in Europe, he returned to the United States, and then baseball, when he joined the Puerto Rican League during the winter of 1945–46.

Upon hearing that Pasquel was sniffing around for players to fill Mexican rosters in 1946—and that he once again had his eye on Irvin—Effa wrote a letter to her former star and begged him to rejoin the Eagles. Her main selling point? Playing in Newark would put Irvin in the best position to make the jump to the Majors.

I believe more Major League teams will take Negro's [sic], however the men they take will have to be good, and there is no doubt you would be one of the men they would want.

This is one of the important reasons why you should play in America this year, so you can be seen for one thing. If the experiment with Negro's [sic] in the Majors is successful, all the teams will be ready to take you …

Whatever you do now will decide you[r] entire future and I hope you make the right move.

As questions around integration continued to swirl, Effa focused her energy into building the best baseball team in Newark Eagles history.

It's unclear whether it was Effa's persuasive pitch or the chance to be back in New Jersey and closer to family that persuaded Irvin to return to the Eagles. All that mattered to Effa was that he did.

*** *** ***

Even without pitcher Don Newcombe, who was preparing to play for Branch Rickey's minor-league Nashua Dodgers, Effa felt that her Eagles were the Negro National League team to beat in '46. And based on the team's home-opening performance, she was right.

The May 5, 1946, contest between the Eagles and the visiting Philadelphia Stars was a mound battle between two of the league's best hurlers.

Future Hall of Famer Leon Day pitched for the Eagles. The twenty-nine-year-old ace was reserved in personality and pitch delivery—he famously threw without a windup—but his wicked curveball and ninety-mile-an-hour-plus fastball spoke volumes. Day squared off against the Stars' Barney Brown, a left-handed pitcher who was popular in Latin American leagues and known for his deadly screwball.

Through five and a half innings, the score was deadlocked at zero, with neither the Eagles nor the Stars able to put points on the scoreboard. One by one, Newark and Philly players stepped into the batter's box, took their swings…and then walked back to the dugout, defeated.

Finally, in the bottom of the sixth, the home team scored two, and the Eagles fans in Ruppert Stadium rose to their feet.

The Stars had a chance to respond in the ninth, when a walk from Day and an error by nineteen-year-old rookie shortstop Benny Felder allowed two men to reach base. Representing the go-ahead run, Henry McHenry, a six-foot-tall Stars pitcher doing double duty as a pinch hitter, approached the plate. A hush fell across the grandstands as fans looked on in anxious silence.

First, Day whizzed a fastball over the heart of the plate. McHenry swung... and missed.

Strike one.

Moments later, another fastball from Day... and another whiff from McHenry.

Strike two!

Then, the final pitch to secure an Eagles victory: Day threw his third fastball, and once again, McHenry's bat connected with nothing but the crisp spring air.

The final score was 2–0, and Day had logged the first no-hitter of his career.

"It was really a beauty," Effa proudly wrote in a letter to sportswriter Art Carter. "Can you imagine what a thrill that was[?]"

The thrills would continue for Effa and her club. Newark notched a ten-game winning streak in June, scored thirty-one runs in a July exhibition game, and won fourteen games in a row through August and September. At the end of the season, there were five Eagles players with batting averages above .300, including Monte Irvin and his league-leading .395; from the mound, pitcher Rufus Lewis was named Rookie of the Year, while Leon Day tallied a

Outfielder Monte Irvin (*left*) and second baseman Larry Doby (*right*) were two of the best players on the 1946 Eagles team that soared to first place in the Negro National League standings.

stellar season-long record of 11–4. Most important of all, the Eagles had clinched the Negro National League title.

Effa was ecstatic. After twelve years in baseball, her team had finally won the pennant, and they had done so quite decisively. Still, she wasn't satisfied, and she wouldn't be until her Eagles were crowned Negro World Series champions.

The Eagles needed to win just four more games in the best-of-seven World Series. But to do so, they'd have to defeat Satchel Paige and the mighty Kansas City Monarchs.

✳✳✳

For Effa Manley and the Newark Eagles, Game 1 of the Negro World Series did not go as planned.

Despite playing in front of a near-home crowd at the Polo Grounds in New York, Effa's team lost 2–1 in a contest that was way too close for comfort. Frustration clouded the air on the bus ride back to New Jersey, but the players refused to let it suffocate them. Two nights later, on Thursday, September 19, they would be ready to redeem themselves.

The Eagles hosted the Monarchs in Newark, and Effa could only hope that playing in their home stadium would improve their fortunes. To ensure a packed house, Effa called on her friend, the boxing icon Joe Louis, to throw out the first pitch. Meanwhile, to provide extra motivation for the players, Newark Mayor Vincent Murphy offered twenty-five dollars to the first Eagle to score a run, and another twenty-five dollars to the first Eagle to hit a homer.

Game 2 was another nail-biter, with the score tied at 1 through five innings. Then, in the top of the sixth, Monarchs outfielder Willard "Home Run" Brown stepped to the plate and fully embodied his alias. He launched a three-run homer over the Ruppert Field fence, putting the Monarchs up 4–1 and sending Effa's heart into her stomach.

Though the Eagles were unable to answer in the bottom of the sixth, they did keep the Monarchs off the board in the top of the next inning before batting their way back into the game after the seventh-inning stretch.

First, Doby smashed a two-run homer four hundred feet over the right-field wall to bring the Eagles to within one. Sensing trouble ahead, the Monarchs pulled their starting pitcher, Ford Smith, and replaced him with the venerable Paige, but not even he could hold off the Eagles' surge. Effa's boys smacked four singles and, with the help of two Monarchs errors, put a total of six runs on the board in the bottom of the seventh inning. The Eagles' scoring drive didn't just put them ahead of the Kansas City team; it put the game out of reach. With their 7–4 victory at home, the Eagles had won their first World Series game and tied the Monarchs at one win apiece.

The teams headed to Blues Stadium in Kansas City for the next two games, which brought even more back-and-forth action. The Eagles lost Game 3 15–5 before winning Game 4 with a score of 8–1. Like Game 1, Game 5 was also held at a neutral field; this time it was Chicago's Comiskey Park, home of the Chicago White Sox and the Negro Leagues' East-West Classic. Kansas City won that game, too, pulling ahead in the series with a three-games-to-two lead over Newark.

With Games 6 and 7 approaching, Effa, and every player on her team, knew it was do or die. The Eagles would have to win Game 6 to stay alive and Game 7 to become the champions. There could be no more errors, no lackluster fielding or lazy batting. This was it.

Game 6 took place on Friday, September 27, at Ruppert Stadium, and from the beginning, Willard "Home Run" Brown seemed dead set on closing out the series with a Monarchs win. He went yard again, smashing a three-run homer in the top of the first inning.

Falling behind that early in the game could have meant certain doom for the Eagles; thankfully, they countered with four runs in the bottom half of the first, driven in on singles from first baseman Lennie Pearson and catcher Charles Ruffin. That was enough to keep the Eagles' offense rolling, and with two homers from Irvin and one from Pearson, the Newark team added five more runs to their total.

When the final scores were tallied, the Eagles had muscled their way to a 9–7 victory over the Monarchs. More important, they'd pushed the 1946 Negro World Series to an all-important Game 7.

CHAMPIONS AT LAST

It was a perfect Sunday for baseball. Though the calendar showed September 29, the weather had yet to break, and the early autumn air was still warm and slightly humid. Ruppert Stadium was electric under the high afternoon sun, as fans from around the city and visitors, too, gathered to cheer on the Eagles, Effa's beloved Eagles, who were just one win away from becoming Negro World Series champions.

But Effa's team wasn't the only one fighting to reach the pinnacle of the baseball world. Just one day before the Eagles' final World Series game, Jackie Robinson and the Montreal Royals topped the Louisville Colonels in Game 1 of the Junior World Series. In his first season in white organized baseball, Robinson had proven that Black players could take the field with white players without incident. He had also proven that, together, they could win.

Notably, the Eagles' opponent, the Kansas City Monarchs, would be missing one of their marquee players for the decisive final game of the series. Satchel Paige, ace pitcher and preeminent showman, had recently embarked on a barnstorming tour with Bob Feller, star hurler for the Cleveland Indians. From the East Coast to the West, tens of thousands of fans of all races were filling bleacher seats to cheer on baseball's best as Paige (and Feller) continued to drive more nails into segregation's coffin.

What Paige wouldn't do, however, was be on hand to help the Monarchs in their Game 7 showdown of the 1946 Negro World Series.

***

All eyes were glued to the field in the bottom of the first inning, when the Eagles' switch-hitting infielder Pat Patterson reached first base on a Monarchs error. Larry Doby drew a walk to move Patterson to second, and a single by Monte Irvin drove him home to put the first run of the game on the scoreboard.

Going into the sixth inning, the Eagles were still on top, but with one sweet swing, Monarchs first basemen John "Buck" O'Neil tied the game with a solo home run.

Effa struggled to keep her heart from bursting through the front of her dress.

In the bottom of the sixth, the Eagles went up 3–1 when Irvin and Doby drew walks and outfielder Johnny Davis batted them in on a line drive double to left field. But Effa couldn't relax for long. The Monarchs scored a run in the top of the seventh to bring the score to 3–2.

It was as if all the air had been sucked out of Ruppert. No way could the Eagles lose the most important game of the season, and on their home field at that. All they had to do was shut down an equally persistent Kansas City team—a team that was eager to wrest the World Series title from Effa's Eagles.

After a scoreless eighth, it all came down to the ninth inning. The first sign of a potential Monarchs comeback came from catcher Mickey Taborn. He hit a sure single with one out, but in a fit of overzealousness, he tried to stretch the hit into a double. Taborn was quickly denied when a throw from Eagles center fielder Jimmy Wilkes stopped him short before he could slide into second base.

Suddenly, there were two outs, and the Monarchs were down to their last life.

Next up to bat was Kansas City pitcher Ford Smith.

He singled.

Then, shortstop Chico Renfroe drew a walk.

Finally, with a man on first and second, Monarchs third baseman Herb Souell took his place at home plate, bat cocked just so.

Every pair of eyes in the stadium was transfixed on the field, all mouths fastened tight in anticipation. Effa was watching from her seat in the press box, her heart rate quickening, her feet making a nervous click-clack pattern on the floor below her.

With the Monarchs' hopes for a championship resting solely on his bat, Souell fouled off a pitch. Instantaneously, the crowd drew a collective sigh of relief. Effa, meanwhile, didn't know how much more she could take. Her entire career—all the contract negotiations and owners' meetings, the game scheduling and promotional activities—had been building to this pivotal moment.

Effa lowered her head, convinced that her nervous system couldn't handle the tension, and in the next moment, she heard it: the sickening crack of bat striking ball.

Effa was afraid to look up. What if Souell had homered? With one swing, he could push the Monarchs to a 5–3 lead, forcing Effa's team to make up the difference in the bottom of the ninth.

But could they do it? The whole game had been close. Too close for Effa's taste, and she didn't know if she could take much more...

But she decided to peek anyway.

Just as she lifted her eyes back to the diamond, Effa saw Lennie Pearson step away from the first-base bag, hold up his glove...and close it around Souell's pop-up. Her gaze then shifted to the umpire standing nearby, who twisted his hand into a fist to declare that Souell was the third out.

And with that, Effa sank back into her seat, drained and unable to move.

The Newark Eagles were Negro World Series champions!

Newark Eagles New Diamond Champs

In a stunning seven-game series, Effa's Eagles defeated the Kansas City Monarchs to become the 1946 Negro World Series champions.

WINNING AND LOSING

The 1946 season couldn't have ended on a higher note for Effa and the Eagles. They were Negro World champions, and prosperous ones, at that. Regarding attendance and revenue, '46 was the best season on record for the Newark team, and as soon as Lennie Pearson snagged the last out of the series, Effa began looking ahead, making plans to duplicate—or even exceed—her team's success in '47. But even as Effa and her Eagles were celebrating, the fractures in Black baseball's white veneer were widening, and Effa's plans would soon be cast aside.

Heading into the 1947 season, the focus of Black fans and sportswriters wasn't on the reigning champions of Black baseball's segregated leagues. It was, instead, on the handful of Black players who had crossed over into white baseball and were slowly, but surely, making a name for themselves.

Jackie Robinson was, of course, leading the pack. He'd become a champion in his own right, first by leading the International League with a .349 batting average and 113 runs scored during the regular season, and then by lifting the Montreal Royals over the Louisville Colonels to claim the 1946 Junior World Series title that fall. In one year, Robinson was able to silence many critics who'd questioned the validity of Rickey's great experiment. He'd also performed well enough to move to the next stage of the process: a Major League debut.

✳✳✳

On April 15, the first day of the 1947 season, Jackie Robinson walked onto the diamond at Ebbets Field as a Brooklyn Dodger and, just as significantly, the first Black man to play Major League Baseball in more than six decades. Over 26,623 fans attended the game, and while the crowd was smaller than the sellout size of thirty-four thousand, remarkably, fourteen thousand ticket holders were Black. They'd come from all across New York to see Robinson

1947 was a history-making year in baseball and all of American society, as Jackie Robinson (*right*) endured relentless racism during his first season with the Dodgers and still went on to earn the Rookie of the Year title.

play, the great Black hope with the navy forty-two on his back, the man who was swinging his way into history books.

Hitting second in the lineup, Robinson's first three at-bats— a grounder to third, a fly ball to left field, and a would-be base hit that Boston Braves shortstop Dick Culler snagged just in time— resulted in outs.

Then, in the bottom of the seventh inning, with the Dodgers losing 3–2, Robinson again stepped into the batter's box as Eddie Stanky, the Dodgers' second baseman, stood on first base. This time, Robinson's mission was clear: He was to lay down a sacrifice bunt that would move Stanky to second, putting him in scoring position as the Braves infield hurried to force Robinson out at first.

Robinson executed the play perfectly. And in a stroke of luck for the Dodgers, Earl Torgeson, the Braves' first baseman who fielded the bunt, did not. After digging the ball out of the dirt, Torgeson swung around to throw Robinson out at first, but the throw was rushed and wild. Instead of landing in his teammate's glove, it hit the sprinting Robinson before rolling away. On the error, Stanky made it all the way to third base while Robinson cruised into second. The two men later scored on a double hit by Dodgers outfielder Pete Reiser.

In the days and weeks following his debut, Robinson had no way of knowing what his baseball legacy would be, especially if his first game was to be any indication. As all of Black America looked to him to represent the race well, Robinson went 0–4 at the plate before being benched for the ninth and final inning. He'd certainly contributed to the team's 5–3 win over the Braves, but according to Robinson's own assessment of his play, he was terrible.

To be clear, it was a miracle that Robinson even made it onto the Dodgers' roster. Johnny Wright, the former Homestead Grays pitcher who had joined Robinson on the minor-league Montreal

Royals for the 1946 season, had been demoted to the Class-C Royals of Three Rivers, Quebec, in May of that year. Sensing that Robinson would still benefit from having a Black teammate in faraway Canada, Rickey hurriedly signed another Negro Leagues pitcher—Roy Partlow, formerly of the Philadelphia Stars—but he also struggled under integration's spotlight.

Despite being signed shortly after Jackie Robinson and joining him on the minor-league Montreal Royals team, the pressure of breaking baseball's color line was too much for pitcher Johnny Wright (*pictured*). In 1947, when Robinson got called up to the big leagues, Wright returned to the Homestead Grays of the Negro National League.

Despite logging a very respectable earned-run average of 2.95 over seven Negro Leagues seasons, Partlow was benched for much of his first two weeks with the Montreal club, further supporting the notion that he was there to do little more than keep Robinson company. When Partlow did take the mound, his game was off and his pitches errant, causing him to suffer the same demotion as Wright.

Partlow wasn't keen on playing for the low-level team in Quebec, though—he'd played against much stiffer competition in the Negro Leagues, and had been dominant—so before he reported to the small Canadian town, Partlow ran off to New York, presumably in an attempt to abandon his Dodgers contract altogether. He did eventually rejoin the team in Three Rivers to finish out the '46 season, but not before Wendell Smith took him to task in the pages of the *Pittsburgh Courier.*

In his July 20 column, Smith wrote little of the intense burden that Partlow must have carried while in Montreal. Instead, he accused the pitcher of not thinking about "those 14 million Negroes from coast to coast who are pulling for him to make good in white organized baseball":

> [Partlow] should recognize the fact that if he quits, there are thousands of people who will clap their hands in glee and say: "See, I told you Negro players can't take it in white organized baseball." They will make such statements, despite the fact that Jackie Robinson is the "darling" of the Montreal Royals, and Johnny Wright is doing all right at Three Rivers, Quebec. Partlow, it appears, needs to sit down and think about the significance of his position.

Wright and Partlow both played a key role in helping the Three Rivers Royals win their own pennant in 1946, yet both players eventually returned to the Negro Leagues, likely unwilling to continue shouldering the stresses of integration while on a third-rate ball club.

Robinson, however, would remain in organized white baseball.

***

Jackie Robinson eventually came out of his early 1947 slump and went on to win National League Rookie of the Year honors after amassing 12 home runs, 48 RBIs, 175 hits, a .297 batting average, and a league-leading 29 stolen bases. Thanks, in part, to Robinson's turnaround, the Dodgers finished first in the National League standings—just ahead of the second-place St. Louis Cardinals, Branch Rickey's former team—and went on to face the New York Yankees in the '47 World Series.

The Dodgers lost three games to four in a thrilling, down-to-the-wire matchup, but even that post-season heartbreak failed to suppress Brooklyn's excitement after Robinson's first season. It wasn't just his play that was a boon for the organization; their fan base grew in '47, too, along with their revenue. "Money is America's

God," Robinson later wrote, "and business people can dig black power if it coincides with green power, so these fans were important to the success of Mr. Rickey's 'Noble Experiment.'"

Rickey may have anticipated that Black fans would come out in droves to see his new Black star race around the Ebbets infield, but he had no way of knowing how white fans would receive them or how Black fans would react when confronted with blistering racism. Still, he expected those Black fans to have the same response as their new hero—that is, they weren't to respond at all.

As much as Robinson's exploits were seen as an audition of sorts for all Black players who hoped to follow him, the whole Black community was in the midst of its own tryout. They would be allowed into the stadiums of Major League teams, yes, but the environment would be hostile and humiliating. And if they didn't refrain from returning the cruelty of the white fans in attendance, Black fans wouldn't just risk being locked outside the stadium's gates for good. They would also risk the future of other Black Major Leaguers.

In his autobiography, *I Never Had It Made*, Robinson wrote about this unyielding pressure, this higher standard to which Black athlete *and* Black spectator were held:

[Black fans] could have blown the whole bit to hell by act-
ing belligerently and touching off a race riot. That would
have been all the bigots needed to set back the cause of pro-
gress of black men in sports another hundred years. I knew
this. Mr. Rickey knew this. But this never happened.

It may have taken a while for Robinson to hit his stride as a player, but from the very first game of the 1947 season, Rickey and the rest of the Dodgers brass could see clearly that Black athletes— and their docile, nonconfrontational followers—would be great for business. Due in part to the unrelenting support Robinson received from the Black community, Brooklyn's 1.8 million tickets sold at home and 1.9 million sold on the road set National League records that year.

Unfortunately, what was great for the Majors proved fatal for the Negro Leagues.

＊＊＊

The Eagles kicked off the '47 season by hosting preseason exhibition games across the South, and Effa was overjoyed at the crowds of fans who came out to see the champions of Black baseball grace the diamond. Tickets were selling, the Manleys were making money, and the Eagles were proving that they were, in fact, the best. Everything was perfect, the manifestation of Effa's biggest and brightest dreams.

Then the regular season began.

Newark performed well and finished the first half of the season in first place. But the crowds—and with them, the ticket sales—collapsed like a house built on sand in the swirling bands of a monster hurricane. Overnight, it seemed, the Eastern Seaboard had become Jackie Robinson Country, and fans who had the option of attending a Negro Leagues game or a contest featuring Number Forty-Two were more often choosing the latter. Effa estimated that the Eagles lost $22,000 that year, as teams all across the NNL considered themselves lucky if they could convince even a couple thousand people to show up for a game.

Even worse, their troubles were only beginning.

✳✳✳

Although it would take some Major League executives more than a decade to add even one Black player to their rosters—the Boston Red Sox were the last team to integrate, in 1959—others were eager to follow Branch Rickey's lead.

Like Rickey, Bill Veeck had spent countless hours in search of a Black player with the right combination of on-the-field prowess and off-the-field maturity to add to his all-white Cleveland Indians. And like Rickey, Veeck turned to the Negro Leagues—to Effa's Eagles, in particular—to find his man.

THE CALL

Few knew it at the time, but Cleveland Indians owner Bill Veeck had considered integrating Major League Baseball in 1942, a full three years before Branch Rickey met with Jackie Robinson and signed him to the Brooklyn Dodgers organization. Veeck owned the minor-league Milwaukee Brewers then, but his secret plan was to purchase the basement-dwelling Philadelphia Phillies and transform them into an all-Black club in Major League Baseball's National League.

To accomplish this, Veeck wanted to host two training camps in the spring of '43: one for a group of white players whom fans and media would expect to take the field for the Phillies that season...

and one for a group of all-stars from the Black baseball world who would make up Philly's *real* roster.

Veeck had long been a fan of the Negro Leagues; he also had a close relationship with Abe Saperstein, founder of the all-Black Harlem Globetrotters basketball team and frequent booking agent for Negro Leagues games. Veeck turned to Saperstein, as well as Fay Young, sports editor of the Black *Chicago Defender* newspaper, to round up the best Black players for his team.

With the pieces of his puzzle coming together, Veeck then scheduled a meeting with Gerry Nugent, the president of the Phillies. Over a handshake, the two men agreed that Veeck would buy the team. The next, and final, step was securing the necessary financing. Once that was completed, Veeck alerted Commissioner Kenesaw Landis to his plans. And this, he wrote in his autobiography, *Veeck as in Wreck*, was his "bad mistake."

Out of my long respect for Judge Landis I felt he was entitled to prior notification of what I intended to do. I was aware of the risk I was taking although, to be honest, I could not see how he could stop me. The color line was a "gentleman's agreement" only. The only way the

Commissioner could bar me from using Negroes would be
to rule, officially and publicly, that they were "detrimental
to baseball." With Negroes fighting in the war, such a rul-
ing was unthinkable.

Veeck wrote that Landis wasn't totally surprised by his plan. After all, it had been less than a year since Landis had publicly stated that Major League owners were free to sign whomever they wanted to their rosters. But according to Veeck, when he let Landis know that he was planning to do just that, the commissioner wasn't happy about it.

Not long after Veeck's meeting, he received word that the Phillies team he was planning to purchase had been sold to a lumber dealer named William Cox—and at a price that was about half of what Veeck was willing to pay.

He never had any proof, but Veeck believed that the commissioner had broken up his plan to buy the Phillies in 1942 simply because he wanted to keep baseball's color line firmly in place. But in 1947, things were much, much different. With Landis dead and Rickey and Robinson showing the baseball world that integration could drive both wins and ticket sales, Veeck knew that nothing could stop him from signing a Black player to his Cleveland club.

He also knew just the player he wanted to sign.

✳✳✳

Effa was enjoying a rare Eagles off day in the early summer of 1947 when Abe walked into the office, his face awash in confusion. "Bill Veeck is going to call you soon," he said.

Immediately, Effa's countenance matched her husband's. "What's it about?"

"It's about Larry Doby," Abe replied. "Veeck's interested in buying him."

It took a few days for Veeck to call. In the meantime, Effa had a lot to think about. She felt sad about letting Doby go; he was one of her best players, of course, but he was like family to the Manleys, too. Doby had even named Abe and Effa the godparents of his oldest son.

Effa was going to miss Doby, but she was also confident that he would be okay in the big leagues. He was a solid player, and she knew he had a long, prosperous career ahead of him. Of her own Eagles team, she wasn't quite so sure.

The effect of having even one player leave Black baseball for the Majors was already obvious. If Robinson gave way to Doby, and then a dozen or more other players followed, how could the Black teams ever survive?

When Veeck finally called, he wasted no time getting to the matter at hand. "Mrs. Manley," he said. "I want to make a deal for your Larry Doby."

Effa took a deep breath. This was the moment she had been waiting, and preparing, for.

"Well, Mr. Veeck, if Larry has a chance to play for your club, I certainly won't stand in his way." She took a pause before adding, "What do you plan to give me for him?"

"A scout of mine, Bill Killefer, has been watching Doby [for] some time. We've come to the conclusion that he's about ready for the big leagues." Now it was Veeck's turn to pause. "I'll give you $10,000 for him."

Effa kept her voice steady. "Well, I'm not a millionaire," she said, "but I am financially secure, and ten thousand dollars looks like ten cents to me. I know very well that if he was a white boy and a free agent, you'd give him $100,000 to sign with you merely as a bonus."

Effa pressed the phone to her ear and counted off a few beats.

One...two...three.

While she waited, Veeck was probably sitting slack-jawed, taken aback by the brashness of a woman who dared to play a man's game—and who played to win.

Truth be told, Effa was in a difficult position. She couldn't respond too quickly to Veeck's offer and appear anxious, like she didn't know how to handle a proper negotiation. Neither did she want to wait so long to reply that Veeck would retract his offer. Doby was like a son to her, and as much as she wished the circumstances were different, she wouldn't dare put his chance to play for the Indians at risk. Even more, Effa didn't want Veeck to grow so frustrated with her hardballing that he decided to steal Doby away like Rickey had stolen Robinson and Newcombe.

Effa simply wanted Veeck to respect her as he would any other team owner, Black or white, male or female.

"I realize I'm in no position to be bargaining with you," Effa said finally. "So if you feel you're being fair by offering us $10,000... I suppose we should accept."

Effa awaited Veeck's verbal agreement, the final okay that would send her Eagles team spinning into the unknown. But first, Veeck offered a compromise. "I'll do this much in your case," he

Like Branch Rickey of the Brooklyn Dodgers, Cleveland Indians owner Bill Veeck (*left*) would become known for leading the push for baseball's integration. Unlike Rickey, who tended to ignore Black players' contracts with Negro Leagues teams, Veeck paid the Manleys for Larry Doby (*right*) when he signed him in the summer of 1947.

said. "If we keep Doby thirty days from the time we sign him up, I'll send you an additional five grand, which will make the total come to $15,000."

Considering Doby's prowess, the extra $5,000 was all but guaranteed. All Effa had to do was get final clearance from Abe.

"I must tell you," she told Veeck, "my husband and I are full partners in this business. He's in Washington, where our team is playing. I'll have to call him first before I can give you any commitment."

Effa hung up and quickly called Abe to relay the conversation. Abe was not impressed. Not only did he feel that $10,000, or even

$15,000, was much too low for a player of Doby's caliber, he feared what would happen to the team's morale if Doby left them in the middle of the season.

Considering all the money the Manleys had invested in developing players—money that they couldn't afford to lose now that ticket sales were on the decline—Abe had a point. But they had no choice but to accept Veeck's offer, whether he paid $10,000 for Doby or $10. If they didn't, Effa told Abe, "everybody would start claiming that we were denying him his greatest break."

Ultimately, Abe agreed, and Effa called Veeck back to let him know.

"There's one more thing I want to take up with you," she said before ending the conversation. "Please promise me you'll never pay Larry less than $5,000 a year. We're paying him about $4,000 right now, and I don't want to think that he would get any less than that."

Veeck promised to meet this final demand, and, with that, Effa cleared the way for Doby to become the first Black player to play in Major League Baseball's American League.

Doby played his first game with the Indians on July 5, 1947. Unlike Robinson, who spent his first year with the Dodgers on a minor-league team, Doby made his debut with Cleveland's

On July 5, 1947, Larry Doby became the second Black player on a Major League roster—and the first on an American League team—when he took the field with the Cleveland Indians.

big-league club. The former Eagle struggled that first season, logging just 5 hits in 32 at-bats over 29 games, but his signing was historic nonetheless.

Across America, Black people had another reason to cheer, another reason to believe that all of racism's walls would soon come tumbling down. As for other Black baseball players, Doby's success was theirs, his footprints representing one more path for the luckiest Negro Leaguers to follow.

But back in Newark, within the walls of the Eagles' main office, Doby's departure meant something entirely different. Now that he was gone and the color line had been crossed in both the Major Leagues, the demise of Effa's team felt all but imminent.

THE BEGINNING
OF THE END

Larry Doby's last games with the Eagles were played in a double-header on July 4, 1947. And as he blasted his fourteenth home run of the season and solidified his .414 batting average, there was no doubt in anyone's mind that he would be missed. "There was little hustle, little inspiring play of any type—even from some of our proud veterans," Effa wrote about the Eagles' first few games without him. "It seems that all of the players were heartbroken that they, too, had not been selected—like Doby—by some Major League club."

Abe, it seemed, had been right.

Still, the '47 season wasn't a total bust. The Eagles weren't able to repeat their pennant-winning performance of 1946, but the team did lead the NNL with seventy home runs, largely because of the sixteen contributed by Monte Irvin. Irvin became the league's individual home run champion, while also leading the NNL in runs batted in with sixty-nine. His teammates stepped up, too: First baseman Lennie Pearson's eighteen doubles were good enough for league best, as were the sixteen wins logged by pitcher Max Manning.

Effa wanted to rejoice in the Eagles' achievements, but she couldn't. Not completely, anyway. Not when her business was disintegrating at warp speed.

After drawing 120,293 fans to Ruppert Stadium in 1946, during the Eagles' championship season, the total attendance for 1947 dropped to a paltry 57,100—and that's including a record-breaking opening-day crowd of 12,552. Of the Eagles' 1947 season, Negro Leagues historian James Overmyer wrote: "If more people had come to see them play, it would have been a perfectly creditable year."

But the crowds weren't coming, and in 1947, Effa was once again thinking about calling it quits. All Black teams were suffering, and there was no relief in sight.

When Tom Wilson and J. B. Martin had met with MLB

commissioner Happy Chandler in early 1946 to discuss forming an official alliance between the Negro Leagues and organized white baseball, only one Black player had been signed. Within months, though, Branch Rickey signed four more Black players; a year later, Bill Veeck came calling for Larry Doby.

As a result, the condition of Black baseball was no longer a priority for the commissioner or any other white baseball executives. If nothing else, Robinson's achievements proved what Rickey had believed all along: There was no need for the Majors to cooperate with Negro Leagues owners to successfully integrate their white teams. Major League owners and executives could simply take what they wanted—the best Black athletes available—and leave behind what they didn't—the Black owners, executives, and coaches, and even the Black players who were past their playing prime or just not good enough to make the jump.

To make matters worse, Effa and the other Negro Leagues owners couldn't even afford to fight against the impenetrable force of white baseball. They were struggling just to survive.

After becoming a key player in the push for integration, as well as a vocal critic of Black baseball's owners, the *Pittsburgh Courier's*

Wendell Smith called for the continued backing of Black baseball in his May 3, 1947, column:

> It is more important now that we support Negro baseball than ever before. For it was that orphan of the diamond world that produced Robinson and it had produced many others who didn't get the break that Rickey gave Jackie. If some other owner decides to copy the boss of Brooklyn and clutch a Negro player to his bosom, it is almost a certainty that the player will come from Negro baseball . . .
>
> Owners of Negro teams deserve consideration, too. After all, they have made big investments and are risking a good bag full of dough each season . . . Some of these owners aren't wholly in support of this campaign to get more Negro players into the majors. But we'll forgive 'em and go along with 'em because they can't do anything about it anyway.

Yet even as Smith claimed to rally around the struggling Negro Leagues, his actions told a different story. He had long stopped covering Black baseball with the same intensity he did during the pre-integration glory days. Instead, his column's ink was dedicated to the exploits of Jackie Robinson, Roy Campanella, and Don Newcombe—the Black players now dressing out for white teams.

Smith's call for support was also too little too late, but once again, Abe persuaded Effa to give Black baseball one more chance.

✳✳✳

"The year 1948 was the same story [as 1947]—but worse, if that's at all possible," Effa wrote in her memoir. "The crowds were just as small, the overall interest just as minimal. Expenses, naturally, went on the same as usual, in spite of a dwindling box office."

Indeed, payroll still had to be met, and there wasn't much owners could do to cut down their budgets. Smith, unsurprisingly, continued to blame the owners, who he thought were paying too much for player salaries and being unrealistic about the business of Black baseball. He didn't comment on the fact that player salaries had gone up because of the increased profits and higher demand for talent during the war years, nor did he consider that players who may have already been upset about not getting a call from the Majors certainly wouldn't have been happy if they were also faced with a sudden decrease in pay.

Critiques like Smith's hit hard. Effa had always seen the Negro

Leagues as a viable enterprise, one that could absolutely compete with the Majors—if the Black community could stick together, that is. And it wasn't just Black sportswriters and fans who Effa believed had turned their backs on Black baseball. With her business crumbling at her feet, Effa was surprised to pick up the June 1948 issue of the Black-owned *Ebony* magazine and find that Jackie Robinson himself had denigrated the very institution that gave him his start:

> My five short months experience in Negro baseball convinced me that the game needs a housecleaning from top to bottom. I found plenty wrong before Brooklyn Dodgers' scout Clyde Sukeforth convinced me to give up my $100-a-week shortstop job with the Monarchs and accept a railroad ticket for a tryout with the Flatbush team. The bad points range all the way from the low salaries paid players and sloppy umpiring to the questionable business connections of many of the team owners.

Robinson went on to criticize Negro Leagues teams for playing exhibition games during the spring instead of training, even though he acknowledged that the teams needed the money earned from those contests. He also mentioned the hectic schedule played by Black teams, which included "[making] the jump between cities in uncomfortable busses and [playing] in games while half asleep and very tired." He didn't point out that Black teams were often at the mercy of white stadium owners when scheduling games, and that the uncomfortable travel could be attributed as much to discriminatory laws as it could any team's travel accommodations.

Later in his essay, Robinson again remarked that the salaries paid to Monarchs players were "low for baseball," though, in his autobiography, *I Never Had It Made*, he referred to his $400-a-month salary with the Monarchs as a "financial bonanza." With age comes wisdom and reflection, and Robinson's autobiography, published more than twenty years after his scathing *Ebony essay*, clearly illustrates his personal journey as a civil rights hero. Indeed, Robinson's words in 1972 convey a humility—a heartache, even—that wasn't publicly present in 1948:

> *Today, as I look back on the opening game of my first World Series, I must tell you that it was Mr. Rickey's drama and that I was only a principal actor. As I write this twenty years later, I cannot stand and sing the anthem.*

I cannot salute the flag; I know that I am a black man
in a white world. In 1972, in 1947, at my birth in 1919,
I know that I never had it made.

Robinson may not have had it made in 1948, but that didn't stop him from comparing the Negro Leagues to the Majors, or from castigating Black baseball for its failure to measure up.

Effa wasn't having it, though, and she didn't hesitate to respond publicly to Robinson's disrespect:

I charge Jackie Robinson with being ungrateful. He is
where he is today because of organized Negro baseball.
I believe that he never would have been noticed if it were
not for the people and the teams he derides.

＊＊＊

The continued division in the Black sports community and a disastrous 1948 season—according to Effa, the Eagles lost $25,000 and saw only thirty-five thousand fans visit Ruppert Stadium—dealt the final blows to the Newark team. The Eagles finished third in the Negro National League standings that season, but it wasn't enough. Not anymore.

In September, Effa and Abe agreed to pull the plug on their once-storied franchise, and under the headline BASEBALL'S GLAMOUR GIRL BOWS OUT...Smith bid farewell:

Effa Manley, the beauteous boss of the Newark Eagles is divorcing baseball because of "mental cruelty and indignities"...

With attendance and profits down in the post-integration Negro Leagues, Abe and Effa had no choice but to sell their Newark Eagles team.

There are many of us, however, who will miss the "Queen of Newark" because despite the fact that she tried to tell us how and what to write, she was always good copy...

Despite her riotous threats and growling when things didn't go her way, Mrs. Manley was every inch a fine, dignified lady and extremely emotional...

Mrs. Manley always said she'd stay in baseball and take the hard knocks with the good. She said somebody had to keep Negro baseball going, keep it alive. That was back in the war days when her Eagles were out-drawing the white team that owned the park she rented. That was back in the days when discriminatory baseball was a profitable venture; back in the days when such greats as Satchel Paige and Josh Gibson were mighty drawing cards and were the "sweethearts" of the owners.

But now that's all over. The well has run dry. It's a new day and an entirely new structure has to be built around Negro baseball. It must be sound, practical and in no way lavish.

The old days have gone.

So has gracious, charming, eccentric Effa Manley. The boys in the press box are gonna miss her—tears and all!

It wasn't Effa's style to go quietly or quickly fade from view, so she made her own public statement, published just days after Smith's highly patronizing September 18 column.

"Baseball is a rich man's game," Effa told a reporter for the *New York Age*. "[Former Yankees' owner Jacob] Ruppert had his beer, [Cubs' owner William] Wrigley had his gum, Abe and I have only each other. I am not worried about myself, but I am concerned about the 400 men and their families who depend on the Negro Leagues and who have suffered by the low gates the leagues have encountered during the past two years."

EFFA'S LAST STAND

Soon after Effa announced that the Eagles were pulling out of the Negro National League, the New York Black Yankees and Homestead Grays followed suit. It was a bitter way for Effa and Abe to close up shop, but they saw no reasonable alternative. There was, however, one last chance to make some cash as they said goodbye to baseball.

With the Eagles, Black Yankees, and Grays out of the NNL, only three teams remained—so few that the Negro American League decided to absorb them for the 1949 season. The NAL teams, mostly in the Midwest, had been less affected by the mass exodus of Black fans to Jackie Robinson's games in and around

Brooklyn. And while teams like the Monarchs would eventually meet a fate similar to that of the Eagles and other eastern teams, they decided to keep playing as long as possible.

The reinforced Negro American League ensured that Black baseball games would continue for at least another season, and with that news, two Memphis businessmen, Dr. W. H. Young and Dr. B. B. Martin—brother of Negro American League President J. B. Martin—saw an opportunity. They offered to pay the Manleys $15,000 for all the Eagles' assets before moving the team to Houston.

The Manleys agreed to the deal, which included a stipulation that if any Major League Baseball team purchased the contract of an Eagles player, the club's new owners would evenly split the proceeds of the sale with the Manleys.

This clause proved critical when, shortly after the Manleys agreed to the sale, Effa read a newspaper article stating that Branch Rickey had signed Monte Irvin to the Dodgers. Effa immediately reached out to Irvin, and he confirmed the report.

Like the rest of the baseball world, Irvin had learned from the media that the Eagles were disbanding. He did not know, however, that the Eagles, and all player contracts, had been sold to new owners. Irvin simply believed he was a free agent and, upon being approached by Dodgers scouts, "didn't hesitate, since [he didn't] have too many years left to play."

Effa understood Irvin's reasoning, but she also understood business. If Irvin had indeed signed with a Major League team, both the Manleys and the new Memphis owners would be entitled to compensation. "Abe and I came to the mutual conclusion that the time had arrived when we could no longer go along with Rickey's obvious attitude of playing our Negro Baseball business interests so cheaply," she wrote in her memoir.

***

The Manleys hired an attorney who reached out to Rickey with evidence that Irvin was still contractually bound to the Eagles. Rickey replied that, like Irvin, he had read newspaper reports and assumed that the team had disbanded. But if Irvin was under contract, Rickey added, he would be promptly released.

Rickey's response wasn't what Effa was hoping for—a check for Irvin's contract would have been nice—but Rickey was always known to play hardball.

So, too, was Effa.

As backlash from the Black press, Black baseball fans, and

Irvin himself began to mount, Effa ignored claims that she was preventing the future Hall of Famer from pursuing his Major League dreams. Instead, she got to work shopping him to the best available bidder.

The Yankees were certainly well aware of Irvin's talent—he'd played many games right in their own ballpark—but they were still six years from integrating and turned Effa away immediately. The next stop was the New York Giants. Unlike the Yankees, they were ready to sign their first Black player.

For her final business deal in professional baseball, Effa arranged the sale of Monte Irvin's contract to the New York Giants of the National League.

"The Giants promptly offered us $5,000 for Monte's contract, and we just as promptly accepted," Effa wrote. "We realized that such a sum was ridiculous for a player of Monte Irvin's caliber, but we realized we were hardly in a position to quibble. More important, we were convinced that such a successful action as we had just concluded with the Giants could—and would—serve as a precedent setter."

And so it was that even as Effa was making her last stand as a baseball mogul, she was also thinking of the other owners of Black baseball teams. Because of her, many Negro Leagues owners were able to demand payment for their own players as they struggled to survive during the last days of Black baseball.

Meanwhile, Effa made good on her agreement with Young and Martin of Memphis. After deducting the attorney's half of the proceeds, the Manleys split the other half with the new Eagles owners, leaving Abe and Effa with $1,250.

The money the Manleys made from the sale of Irvin's contract was but a fraction of the $100,000 that Effa estimated they'd lost during their time in the Negro Leagues, but it represented so much more. The money was justification—for all the fighting, the speaking out, the going against the grain. And it was validation, too. It was validation for Effa's very presence in an industry that was kind to neither women nor Black people, and certainly not to those who dared to be both.

So with that in mind, the always stylish Effa—who'd spent nearly two decades working in the fashion industry before ever dipping her perfectly manicured toe into the fierce, yet fabulous, world of professional baseball—decided to use the money from the Giants to buy herself a special gift.

"Abe agreed to allow me to purchase a beautiful mink cape with our fourth portion," wrote the woman who was both of, and *ahead* of, her time. "I still have this cape in my possession, and occasionally I get it out and look at it. It serves to remind me of yet another bit of baseball history in which I have been privileged to play a small role!"

Effa's efforts to save the Negro Leagues from failure may have been unsuccessful, but she will be remembered for her role as the Queen of Black baseball nonetheless.

EPILOGUE

On July 25, 1966, Ted Williams, former Boston Red Sox outfielder and one of the best hitters the game has ever seen, was inducted into the National Baseball Hall of Fame. The honor itself was no surprise; after all, he'd been a nineteen-time All-Star and two-time MVP of the American League. Instead, for the media and fans gathered in Cooperstown, New York, to see the ceremony, it was Williams's induction speech that proved unpredictable.

After thanking former coaches and his team's owner, Williams noted how lucky he'd been to have a career worthy of the Hall of Fame. He then turned his attention to those who'd had equally storied careers, even if they weren't acknowledged at the highest level. "I hope that someday the names of Satchel Paige and Josh Gibson in some way could be added as a symbol of the great Negro players that are not here only because they were not given the chance," Williams told the crowd.

Five years later, in 1971, Paige joined Williams in the annals of Cooperstown, and over the next thirty years, seventeen more former Negro Leaguers were also inducted. It was a noble gesture by the Hall of Fame, but it was still largely inadequate. Anyone paying any attention knew that there were many more than eighteen Negro Leagues players, coaches, and executives deserving of baseball's greatest honor. Indeed, even in death, those Negro Leaguers were facing the same exclusions that haunted them during their lives.

Then, in the summer of 2005, the Hall made an effort to remedy their previous oversights by assembling a special committee of experts and historians to nominate any Negro Leagues participants who were worthy of induction. Ultimately a list of ninety-four was whittled down to seventeen new inductees—including Effa Manley, who became the first woman inducted into the National Baseball Hall of Fame when she was posthumously honored on July 30, 2006.

Sometimes I imagine what Effa would think about our world if she were still alive.

I can see her at her induction ceremony, wrapped tightly in her mink stole despite the summer heat bearing down. I can hear her cheering loudly for the other inductees, including her fellow owners Cum Posey and J. L. Wilkinson, as well as Biz Mackey, who was a faithful player-manager for the Eagles for many years. I can see the pride and joy on her face. But beyond her smile, I can also see layers of frustration.

I know that if Effa were alive today, fifteen years after her induction into Cooperstown, she would be unhappy with the current state of Black people in baseball. She would be angered by the fact that not only do Black players represent just 8 percent of all Major Leaguers, but the number of Black executives in MLB's front offices is also woefully small. And among majority owners of MLB teams, there are no Black people at all.

I know that Effa would be upset, because I know that as she kicked up dust in Negro National League meetings and raised hell in the pages of the *Pittsburgh Courier* and other Black newspapers, this is the reality that she was hoping to avoid. She knew that Black players, coaches, and executives were immensely talented, but she also knew that as Branch Rickey and others chose to exploit that talent while simultaneously stripping it of any power or authority, the impact would be felt for generations.

Still, I also believe that if Effa were alive today, she would have the utmost faith that we, as a society, could be the change we want to see. In the same way that Rube Foster, Gus Greenlee, and others created opportunities for Black players where there were none, we now have the power to create similar opportunities—both in and outside of sports—where they remain nonexistent.

Truly, if Effa's story—of forging her path in a male-dominated industry while tirelessly advocating for both Black baseball and Black people—reveals nothing else, it teaches us this: We are more powerful than we know.

AUTHOR'S NOTE

The book that you are holding is more than fifteen years in the making.

The journey began in 2004, when I accepted the job of marketing assistant at the Negro Leagues Baseball Museum in Kansas City, Missouri. I wasn't planning on writing a book back then; I had just graduated with a degree in sport management, and the museum was a planned pit stop on my way to a position in the front office of a Major League Baseball team. Then, on my first day of work, I was given a tour of the exhibit that changed my life forever.

The museum is designed chronologically; visitors walk along the time line of Black baseball, beginning with the "gentleman's agreement" that forced Black players out of organized baseball in the 1880s and ending in the 1950s, when the post–Jackie Robinson Negro Leagues were hanging on by a thread. As I walked through the exhibit, the stories of men like Satchel Paige and Josh Gibson were obviously fascinating. But with my dream of becoming the first woman general manager of an MLB team fastened tightly in my heart, it was the owners and executives of the Negro Leagues who intrigued me most.

I learned about Effa Manley midway through that first tour. I learned that while she co-owned the Newark Eagles with her husband, Abe, it was Effa who handled all the team's business operations, despite having no prior baseball experience. Suddenly, and for the first time, my own career goals felt achievable.

Aside from the fuel it provided for my adult aspirations, Effa's is the story I wish I'd had earlier, when I was the lone Black face in advanced placement classes, when the limited Black history I was taught depicted us, most often, as either slaves or victims of Jim Crow's water hoses and billy clubs. I didn't realize it then, but between Emancipation and the civil rights movement, whole decades of Black trial and Black triumph had been swallowed by a chasm of white narrative.

Because discussions about Black baseball tend to focus on the individual players, rarely do we consider the savvy entrepreneurs who built the leagues and teams that made their play possible. Neither do we examine the role of baseball's integration in the death of the Negro Leagues, or how that fatal blow rendered Black coaches and executives, including Effa, jobless. Even now, despite the "progress" that followed Jackie's signing, the Black community remains woefully underrepresented in the front offices of pro teams across all sports.

My purpose in writing this book was not to tell you how I think you should feel about the decisions made by those who have come before. Instead, my goal was to lay all the facts on the table, unnerving as they may be, and to encourage you to have tough conversations about tough situations. At the same time, I wanted to introduce you to a story that I desperately needed when I was your age. It is a story of heartbreak and broken promises, sure. But more than that, it is a story of grit and ingenuity, courage and victory.

I hope you have enjoyed it.

GOFISH

DISCUSSION QUESTIONS

1. Why was baseball so important to Effa Manley?

2. What were some of the challenges the Black community faced in American cities?

3. What is a baseball team's pitcher-catcher combination called?

4. What were some of the opportunities Black baseball provided to the Black community?

5. Define the term *barnstorming*.

6. What were some ways Rube Foster contributed to the progress of Black baseball?

7. How did living in Harlem shape Effa Manley and her ideals?

8. Why were some Black baseball players persuaded to play in Latin America instead of America? How did Effa feel about how the NNL handled issues of players leaving to join teams in other countries?

9. How did historical events like the Great Depression and World War II affect Black baseball?

10. How did Branch Rickey's 1945 signing of Jackie Robinson to the Dodgers affect the future of Black baseball? Why

was Effa concerned with the way Robinson's signing was handled?

11. How did the pressures of integration affect Black players recruited onto white teams? How were the players expected to respond to these pressures?

SOURCE NOTES

INTRODUCTION

3. "a staggering $700...on the field": Overmyer, *Queen of the Negro Leagues*, 102, 204.

4. "more than...that September night": "Monarch Tops Newark in Negro Series Tilt," *Baltimore Sun*, September 18, 1946; Overmyer, *Queen of the Negro Leagues*, 205.

6. Description of Negro World Series Game 1: "Monarch Tops Newark in Negro Series Tilt," Baltimore *Sun*, September 18, 1946; Overmyer, *Queen of the Negro Leagues*, 205.

6. "despite having...regular season": Bush and Nowlin, *Newark Eagles Take Flight*, ebook, chap. 33, loc. 13443–13460.

8. "Paige hit the ball...second": Bush and Nowlin, *Newark Eagles Take Flight*, ebook, chap. 38, loc. 14470.

CHAPTER 1

15. "Effa's mother...with her boss": Overmyer, *Queen of the Negro Leagues*, 6; Luke, *Most Famous Woman in Baseball*, 1.

15. "Effa was in first grade...she asked": Interview with Effa Manley, Louie B. Nunn Center for Oral History, University of Kentucky Libraries, 1:31:11; Overmyer, *Queen of the Negro Leagues*, 6; Luke, *Most Famous Woman in Baseball*, 2.

17. " 'You tell that woman'...her mother said": Interview with Effa Manley, Louie B. Nunn Center for Oral History, University of Kentucky Libraries,

1:31:11; Overmyer, *Queen of the Negro Leagues*, 6; Luke, *Most Famous Woman in Baseball*, 2.

18. "Throughout her childhood…Black community": Luke, *Most Famous Woman in Baseball*, 3.

CHAPTER 2

20. "The Newarks…Callahan for the visitors": "The Bisons Defeated," *Buffalo (NY) Commercial*, May 3, 1887.

21. "In fact…professional baseball": Mancuso, "May 2, 1887: The first African-American battery," Society for American Baseball Research.

22. "first documented…New York and Brooklyn": Thorn, "October 1845: The first recorded baseball games," Society for American Baseball Research.

22. "During the Civil War…growing fan base": Heaphy, *Negro Leagues: 1869–1960*, 9.

24. Background of Catto/founding of Pythians: Swanson, *When Baseball Went White*, 48–52.

24. "The Pythians won…and Washington, DC": Swanson, *When Baseball Went White*, 42.

24. "So talented…of DC": Swanson, *When Baseball Went White*, 57.

25. "Catto's club…the next century": Swanson, *When Baseball Went White*, 53.

25. "In their most…first governing body": Swanson, *When Baseball Went White*, 103; Heaphy, *Negro Leagues: 1869–1960*, 10.

25. "'It is not presumed…colored persons'": Heaphy, *Negro Leagues: 1869–1960*, 10.

26. "'Some baseball leadership…would be done'": Heaphy, *Negro Leagues: 1869–1960*, 10.

26. "When the NABBP…official documents": Heaphy, *Negro Leagues: 1869–1960*, 10.

27. "Despite these risks…from his wounds": Swanson, *When Baseball Went White*, 144.

27. "Catto's Pythians…his murder": Swanson, *When Baseball Went White*, 148.

28. "He started his career…considered professional": Heaphy, *Negro Leagues:*

1869–1960, 12; Riley, *Biographical Encyclopedia of the Negro Baseball Leagues*, 294–295.

28. "Fowler joined…on the team": McKenna, "Bud Fowler," Society for American Baseball Research.

28. "There were other…quick bat": Hurd, "Sol White," Society for American Baseball Research; McKenna, "Frank Grant," Society for American Baseball Research.

29. "Fleet took…in the lineup": Husman, "Fleet Walker," Society for American Baseball Research; Heaphy, *Negro Leagues: 1869–1960*, 14; Riley, *Biographical Encyclopedia of the Negro Baseball Leagues*, 810–811.

29. "'I had it in…his signals'": "Color Line in Base Ball," *New York Age*, January 11, 1919.

31. Cap Anson and the drawing of baseball's color line: Fleitz, "Cap Anson," Society for American Baseball Research; Husman, "August 10, 1883: Cap Anson vs. Fleet Walker," Society for American Baseball Research; Rosenberg, Howard, "Fantasy Baseball: The Momentous Drawing of the Sport's 19th Century 'Color Line' Is Still Tripping Up History Writers," *Atavist*; Heaphy, *Negro Leagues: 1869–1960*, 14.

CHAPTER 3

33. "Born in 1879…Chicago Union Giants": Odzer, "Rube Foster," Society for American Baseball Research; Riley, *Biographical Encyclopedia of the Negro Baseball Leagues*, 290–292; Cottrell, *Best Pitcher in Baseball*, 9.

34. "Foster's first appearance…only one game": Odzer, "Rube Foster," Society for American Baseball Research.

35. "In an exhibition game…new moniker": Riley, *Biographical Encyclopedia of the Negro Baseball Leagues*, 290.

36. "'When he enters…a certain place'": "Well, Well, Man, Rube Foster Certainly Eats 'Em Alive," *Inter Ocean* (Chicago), August 11, 1907.

36. "although a dispute…with the team": Cottrell, *Best Pitcher in Baseball*, 32.

37. "In 1907…for the players": Cottrell, *Best Pitcher in Baseball*, 41–42.

37. "On the field…best season ever": Odzer, "Rube Foster," Society for American Baseball Research.

38. "By the early 1900s ... city's ballparks": Revel, "Early Pioneers of the Negro Leagues: Nat Strong," Center for Negro League Baseball Research, 2.

39. "In 1907 ... for doing so": Revel, "Early Pioneers of the Negro Leagues: Nat Strong," Center for Negro League Baseball Research, 3.

40. " 'The idea is ... in that manner' ": "New Base Ball League Bobs Up on Horizon," *Philadelphia Inquirer,* October 29, 1906.

41. "In 1908 ... he didn't control": Revel, "Early Pioneers of the Negro Leagues: Nat Strong," Center for Negro League Baseball Research, 5.

CHAPTER 4

43. "Moseley and company ... the Black circuit": Heaphy, *Negro Leagues: 1869–1960,* 30–31; Revel and Munoz, "Early Pioneers of the Negro Leagues: Frank C. Leland," Center for Negro League Baseball Research, 9.

43. "Like most owners ... stayed in place": "In the World of Sport: Trouble in Colored Baseball Leagues—Two Teams on Blacklist," *New York Age,* April 14, 1910; Revel and Munoz, "Early Pioneers of the Negro Leagues: Frank C. Leland," Center for Negro League Baseball Research, 20–21; Heaphy, *Negro Leagues: 1869–1960,* 31.

44. "With his legal background ... off the ground": Heaphy, *Negro Leagues: 1869–1960,* 25–26.

45. "After luring away ... new Comiskey Park": Heaphy, *Negro Leagues: 1869–1960,* 31.

47. " 'In my opinion ... the heading of' ": Lester, *Rube Foster in His Time,* 54–55; Heaphy, *Negro Leagues: 1869–1960,* 35.

47. "From November 1919 ... personal ones": Lester, *Rube Foster in His Time,* 107–113; Cottrell, *Best Pitcher in Baseball,* 142–148.

48. Establishment of the Negro National League: Lester, *Rube Foster in His Time,* 114–115; Heaphy, *Negro Leagues: 1869–1960,* 40–41; Cottrell, *Best Pitcher in Baseball,* 150–152.

50. " 'Gentlemen ... who are present' ": Cottrell, *Best Pitcher in Baseball,* 150.

50. "Players who jumped ... disciplinary action": Heaphy, *Negro Leagues: 1869–1960,* 41.

CHAPTER 5

51. "It was difficult...with applause": "Africa for Africans Is Negro Plan," *Windsor (ON) Star*, August 3, 1920; "15,000 Pledge 'Sacred Blood' to Free Africa," *New-York Tribune*, August 3, 1920; "20,000 Negroes Roar Applause to Demand for Free Africa," *Baltimore Sun*, August 3, 1920; "Negroes Urged to Fight for Africa," *Washington Times*, August 3, 1920.

52. "'We declare'...Garvey shouted": "20,000 Negroes Roar Applause to Demand for Free Africa," *Baltimore Sun*, August 3, 1920.

52. Garvey's background and founding of UNIA: "Marcus Garvey," The Official Website of the Universal Negro Improvement Association and African Communities League, includes "The Negro's Greatest Enemy," an autobiographical statement written by Garvey.

53. Washington's Compromise: On September 18, 1895, Booker T. Washington delivered a speech before a predominately white audience at the Cotton States and International Exposition in Atlanta, Georgia. The speech, which would come to be known as the Atlanta Compromise, clearly illustrates his position on racial progress. "The wisest among my race understand that the agitation of questions of social equity is the extremest folly," he said, "and that progress in the enjoyment of all the privilege that will come to us must be the result of severe and constant struggle rather than of artificial forcing."

54. "In 1916...came, too": Luke, *Most Famous Woman in Baseball*, 3.

54. The history of Harlem: Johnson, James Weldon, "The Making of Harlem," *Survey Graphic* magazine, March 1925 (https://web.archive.org/web/20060615081628/http://etext.virginia.edu/harlem/JohMakiF.html); "History of Harlem," *The Neighborhood Projects of Professor Lobel's Seminar 2*, The City University of New York, 2011.

54. "As developers lamented...the South": "Father of Harlem Called It Home," *New York Age*, June 16, 1991.

55. "'Colored Tenants...our people'": "Father of Harlem Called It Home," *New York Age*, June 16, 1991.

55. "By 1914...'all blacks of prominence'": "Father of Harlem Called It Home," *New York Age*, June 16, 1991.

56. Garvey, Du Bois, and colorism in the Black community: "Colorism as Racism: Garvey, Du Bois and the Other Color Line," *Black Perspectives* blog, African American Intellectual History Society, May 24, 2017.

56. "While Garvey…'Tenth'": Du Bois, W. E. B., "The Talented Tenth." http:// moses.law.umn.edu/darrow/documents/Talented_Tenth.pdf.

58. "Like Du Bois…with darker skin": Luke, *Most Famous Woman in Baseball*, 3.

CHAPTER 6

61. "'So for generations…from without'": Locke, Alain, "Enter the New Negro," *Survey Graphic* magazine, March 1925.

61. "She continued…Harlem socialites": Luke, *Most Famous Woman in Baseball*, 3.

61. "Effa also…a few months": Overmyer, *Queen of the Negro Leagues*, 12; Luke, *Most Famous Woman in Baseball*, 3.

62. "'I was…out of the park'": Overmyer, *Queen of the Negro Leagues*, 8.

63. "By 1923…$150,000 today": Heaphy, *Negro Leagues: 1869–1960*, 48.

63. "including…in 1923": Haupert, "MLB's annual salary leaders since 1974," Society for American Baseball Research.

63. "After all league expenses…as a whole": Heaphy, *Negro Leagues: 1869–1960*, 47–48.

64. "'For 5 per cent…the other clubs'": Lester, *Rube Foster in His Time*, 131–133.

64. "He released some…financial trouble": Cottrell, *Best Pitcher in Baseball*, 153; Heaphy, *Negro Leagues: 1869–1960*, 54.

65. Foster's attempted resignation: "Foster Gives Reasons for Resigning," *Chicago Defender*, December 27, 1924; Heaphy, *Negro Leagues: 1869–1960*, 44.

65. "With Foster serving…Negro Southern League": Heaphy, *Negro Leagues: 1869–1960*, 42; Cottrell, *Best Pitcher in Baseball*, 152.

66. "Ed Bolden…three years later": Haupert, "Ed Bolden," Society for American Baseball Research.

66. Bolden, Foster, and the Eastern Colored League: Haupert, "Ed Bolden," Society for American Baseball Research; Lester, *Rube Foster in His Time*, 151–152.

67. "In response...with white men": "War Clouds Gather as Bolden Defies Authority of 'Rube,'" *Pittsburgh Courier,* January 20, 1923.

68. "The Monarchs won...$52,000": Heaphy, *Negro Leagues: 1869–1960,* 65.

CHAPTER 7

69. Description of Foster's accident: "League Head Is Victim of Leaking Gas," *Pittsburgh Courier,* June 6, 1925; Cottrell, *Best Pitcher in Baseball,* 168; Lester, *Rube Foster in His Time,* 166.

70. "'Two or three...catch him'": Lester, *Rube Foster in His Time,* 166–167.

72. "Foster met...integrated contests": Cottrell, *Best Pitcher in Baseball,* 170.

73. "'We were sitting..."call the law"'": Lester, *Rube Foster in His Time,* 167; Cottrell, *Best Pitcher in Baseball,* 171.

73. "Foster was admitted...Kankakee, Illinois": Lester, *Rube Foster in His Time,* 168–169.

73. "In 1928...from the sale": Lester, *Rube Foster in His Time,* 169; Cottrell, *Best Pitcher in Baseball,* 171–172.

74. Abe's early years: Luke, *Most Famous Woman in Baseball,* 3–4.

75. Abe and Black baseball: Luke, *Most Famous Woman in Baseball,* 4–5.

76. "after being admitted...had ever known": Lester, *Rube Foster in His Time,* 173–175.

77. "'We hesitate...appears toppling'": Lester, *Rube Foster in His Time,* 174.

CHAPTER 8

78. "Abe ran the...numbers racket": Luke, *Most Famous Woman in Baseball,* 4; Overmyer, *Queen of the Negro Leagues,* 9.

78. Numbers running in the Black community: Overmyer, *Queen of the Negro Leagues,* 9–12; Harris, "Playing the Numbers: Madame Stephanie St. Clair and African American Policy Culture in Harlem," *Black Women, Gender and Families* 2, no. 2 (Fall 2008), 53–76.

80. "In the fall of 1932...from Philadelphia": Luke, *Most Famous Woman in Baseball,* 5.

81. "Effa became...Cab Calloway": Luke, *Most Famous Woman in Baseball*, 6; Overmyer, *Queen of the Negro Leagues*, 13–15.

82. "Most notably...Black community": Saint-Arnaud, *African American Pioneers of Sociology*, 180.

82. "When Effa...appeared to be white": Overmyer, *Queen of the Negro Leagues*, 13.

83. "'This code...its people'": Bascom, *Renaissance in Harlem*, 9.

84. "Frustrated...in 1933": Lewis, *W. E. B. Du Bois*, 314–316, 331.

85. "'It must be remembered...the greatest advance'": Lewis, *W. E. B. Du Bois*, 337.

86. "At a dinner...'hire a Negro'": Interview with Effa Manley, Louie B. Nunn Center for Oral History, University of Kentucky Libraries, 1:26:13.

87. "Blumstein's department store...happy to assist": Interview with Effa Manley, Louie B. Nunn Center for Oral History, University of Kentucky Libraries, 1:26:13; Luke, *Most Famous Woman in Baseball*, 7; Overmyer, *Queen of the Negro Leagues*, 16; Sclar, *Beyond Stereotypes*, 22.

88. "In cities...with Blumstein's": Overmyer, *Queen of the Negro Leagues*, 16.

88. "After changing...April 8, 1934": Sclar, *Beyond Stereotypes*, 22.

89. "Over fourteen days...today's dollars": Overmyer, *Queen of the Negro Leagues*, 16.

89. "Receipts in hand...the reverend's request": Overmyer, *Queen of the Negro Leagues*, 17.

90. "For six weeks...eventual success": Sclar, *Beyond Stereotypes*, 23.

CHAPTER 9

92. "For two hours...'Nor are we prepared to'": "Blumstein's to Hire Negro Clerks," *New York Age*, August 4, 1934.

93. "'You know, Mr. Blumstein...telling you what's true'": Interview with Effa Manley, Louie B. Nunn Center for Oral History, University of Kentucky Libraries, 1:26:13.

94. "'In recognition...arrived at today'": "Blumstein's to Hire Negro Clerks," *New York Age*, August 4, 1934.

96. "Although many...middle class": Sclar, *Beyond Stereotypes*, 24.

96. "After the initial...never materialized": Sclar, *Beyond Stereotypes*, 23.

97. "Abe was a player's owner...stats and strategy": Interview with Effa Manley, Louie B. Nunn Center for Oral History, University of Kentucky Libraries, 3:04.

98. "On November 13, 1934...Brooklyn Eagles": Luke, *Most Famous Woman in Baseball*, 9.

98. "Representatives...other Black teams": Overmyer, *Queen of the Negro Leagues*, 32.

99. "In a move...Hall of Fame": Overmyer, *Queen of the Negro Leagues*, 33; Luke, *Most Famous Woman in Baseball*, 12.

100. "'There's a lot...being wasted'": Manley and Hardwick, *Negro Baseball... Before Integration*, 40–41.

CHAPTER 10

103. "Born in Marion...the legal route": Whitaker, *Smoketown*, 91; McKenna, "Gus Greenlee," Society for American Baseball Research.

103. "During the height...Pittsburgh": Whitaker, *Smoketown*, 92.

104. "Hundreds of gamblers...men as runners": Whitaker, *Smoketown*, 94–95.

105. "Greenlee was shrewd...spread the word": Whitaker, *Smoketown*, 96–97.

105. "It was because...ticket sales": Whitaker, *Smoketown*, 98–99; McKenna, "Gus Greenlee," Society for American Baseball Research.

106. "Like Greenlee's...large fleet": McKenna, "Cum Posey," Society for American Baseball Research.

107. "Posey's mother...footsteps": Whitaker, *Smoketown*, 47; McKenna, "Cum Posey," Society for American Baseball Research.

107. Posey the athlete and early days with the Grays: Whitaker, *Smoketown*, 47–48; McKenna, "Cum Posey," Society for American Baseball Research.

CHAPTER 11

111. "During the 1931 season...Satchel Paige": Whitaker, *Smoketown*, 105.

111. Satchel Paige's early life and career: Tye, "Satchel Paige," Society for American Baseball Research.

113. "Pitcher Harry Kincannon...10–7 victory": "Grays Bow in 10–7 Thriller," *Pittsburgh Courier*, August 1931.

113. "Greenlee was so thrilled...agreed to": Whitaker, *Smoketown*, 106.

114. Posey's rules for the East-West League: McKenna, "Cum Posey," Society for American Baseball Research; Whitaker, *Smoketown*, 106–107.

115. "Greenlee's top recruit...join the competition": Whitaker, *Smoketown*, 107; Johnson, "Josh Gibson," Society for American Baseball Research.

117. "Greenlee Field opened...secure the win": McKenna, "Gus Greenlee," Society for American Baseball Research; "Crawfords, Black Yanks Vie Tonight," *Pittsburgh Press*, April 29, 1932; "Crawfords Defeated in Opening Game," *Pittsburgh Press*, April 30, 1932.

117. "Ahead of...$1,600 per month": Heaphy, *Negro Leagues: 1869–1960*, 102–103; McKenna, "Gus Greenlee," Society for American Baseball Research.

CHAPTER 12

122. "'I suppose...completely involved'": Interview with Effa Manley, Louie B. Nunn Center for Oral History, University of Kentucky Libraries, 4:23.

123. Eagles' Opening Day, 1935: Luke, *Most Famous Woman in Baseball*, 13; Overmyer, *Queen of the Negro Leagues*, 34–35; "Grays Put Damper on Eagles' Opener," *Pittsburgh Press*, May 19, 1935; "Brooklyn Eagles Beaten in Opener," *Times Union* (Brooklyn, NY), May 19, 1935.

124. "The Eagles finished...just above .500": 1935 Season, Negro National League II, seamheads.com.

125. "Effa learned...operations": Manley and Hardwick, *Negro Baseball... Before Integration*, 43.

125. "'[Abe] Manley...wanted me'": Holway, *Black Diamonds*, 66.

125. The Eagles and the Puerto Rican League: Overmyer, *Queen of the Negro Leagues*, 37; interview with Effa Manley, Louie B. Nunn Center for Oral History, University of Kentucky Libraries, 38:38.

126. "of all the lessons...baseball profits": Manley and Hardwick, *Negro Baseball... Before Integration*, 46–47.

127. "So when Abe...Newark Eagles": Newman and Rosen, *Black Baseball Black Business*, 77.

127. "The Dodgers had fared...winning percentage": 1935 Season, Negro National League II, seamheads.com.

128. "the People's Finance...of the time": Luke, *Most Famous Woman in Baseball*, 19.

128. "Newark's Black residents...of the era": Overmyer, *Queen of the Negro Leagues*, 51.

129. "During her time...up close": Overmyer, *Queen of the Negro Leagues*, 58–61.

130. "Before moving...stadium lighting": Overmyer, *Queen of the Negro Leagues*, 106–107.

131. "According to historian...better team": Overmyer, *Queen of the Negro Leagues*, 90–91.

CHAPTER 13

132. "By 1937...in the Majors": Overmyer, *Queen of the Negro Leagues*, 53.

132. "Unfortunately...Homestead Grays": 1937 Season, Negro National League II, seamheads.com.

133. "Committed to returning...in 1934": McKenna, "Cum Posey," Society for American Baseball Research.

134. Trujillo's Dragones and the recruitment of Satchel Paige: Tye, *Satchel: The Life and Times of an American Legend*, 108–110.

137. " 'We couldn't stay...all the same' ": Holway, *Black Diamonds*, 59–60.

138. " 'The opportunities...think about' ": Tye, *Satchel: The Life and Times of an American Legend*, 116.

139. "He was happier...of Santiago": Tye, *Satchel: The Life and Times of an American Legend*, 114–115.

139. "Gus Greenlee...perilous situation": Lanctot, *Negro League Baseball*, 61; Tye, *Satchel: The Life and Times of an American Legend*, 110.

139. " 'If they fail...ball-players appear' ": "Crawfords-Grays Renew Old Feud in Negro League Preliminary," *Pittsburgh Press*, May 1, 1937.

139. "On May 25...their agreements": Lanctot, *Negro League Baseball*, 64;

"Morton Asks US State Department to Act on Player 'Steal,'" *Pittsburgh Courier*, May 29, 1937.

141. "Left to their...late July": Lanctot, *Negro League Baseball*, 65.

141. "But the players...of the profits": Lanctot, *Negro League Baseball*, 65–66; Tye, *Satchel: The Life and Times of an American Legend*, 116–117; "Posey's Points," *Pittsburgh Press*, July 31, 1937.

CHAPTER 14

143. "'The writer...without a rudder'": "Posey's Points," *Pittsburgh Courier*, August 14, 1937.

144. "'Mrs. Abe Manley...businesslike manner'": "Naming of Loop President, Sec'y Set for Jan. 19," *Pittsburgh Courier*, January 16, 1937.

145. Birth of the East-West All-Star Classic: Lanctot, *Negro League Baseball*, 22–23.

146. "In 1934...sporting event": Lanctot, *Negro League Baseball*, 38; Heaphy, *Negro Leagues: 1869–1960*, 120.

146. "But despite the strong...key organizers": Overmyer, *Queen of the Negro Leagues*, 128.

147. "'When no one...of the picture'": "Men Who Started 'Dream Game' Idea Won't Fail Fandom," *Pittsburgh Courier*, August 1, 1936.

147. "So they asked...'of the game'": Overmyer, *Queen of the Negro Leagues*, 6; "Posey's Points," *Pittsburgh Courier*, August 21, 1937.

147. "'The proper place'...he said": Lanctot, *Negro League Baseball*, 86.

148. "Just ahead of...(NAL)": Lanctot, *Negro League Baseball*, 59.

148. "But Greenlee...'this office'": "Greenlee Claims Proposed 'World Series' Is Unsanctioned by League," *Pittsburgh Courier*, September 18, 1937.

149. "'difficult...in the world'": Manley and Hardwick, *Negro Baseball... Before Integration*, 49.

150. "Effa estimated...$700,000 today": Manley and Hardwick, *Negro Baseball...Before Integration*, 50–51.

150. "In 1939...the home team": "Attendance Records," Effa Manley Papers, Newark Public Library, August 20, 1939.

151. "'We were proud...in all instances'": Manley and Hardwick, *Negro Baseball...Before Integration*, 50.

151. "'Effa had...her for that'": Holway, *Black Diamonds*, 162.

CHAPTER 15

155. "That all changed...World Series title": "1936 World Series."

155. Powell's racist comments and the ensuing fallout: "Public Slur in 1938 Laid Bare a Game's Racism," *New York Times*, July 27, 2008; "Bigot Unwittingly Sparked Change," ESPN.com, February 21, 2014.

157. "Commissioner Landis...ten games": "Powell Suspended for Radio Remark," *Brooklyn Daily Eagle*, July 31, 1938.

158. "'The big league moguls...a bit cruder'": "Smitty's Sports Spurts," *Pittsburgh Courier*, January 14, 1939.

CHAPTER 16

160. "His finances...two months later": McKenna, "Gus Greenlee," Society for American Baseball Research; Lanctot, *Negro League Baseball*, 78–79.

161. "Tom Wilson...Greenlee's stead": Lanctot, *Negro League Baseball*, 79–80.

161. "In 1937...league teams": Lanctot, *Negro League Baseball*, 111.

162. "On the matter...Ed Bolden": Lanctot, *Negro League Baseball*, 88.

163. "After spending...a profitable team": Haupert, "Ed Bolden," Society for American Baseball Research.

164. "'The promoter...per game'": "Posey's Points," *Pittsburgh Courier*, February 17, 1940.

164. "'We are fighting...race issue'": Lanctot, *Negro League Baseball*, 88.

165. "Effa's decision...'for a lady'": Lanctot, *Negro League Baseball*, 88–89; "Posey's Points," *Pittsburgh Courier*, February 17, 1940.

CHAPTER 17

170. "Even before...global conflict": *Economic Consequences of War on the US Economy*, Institute for Economics and Peace, 7–9.

171. "The Federal Housing Authority...NRA-mandated benefits": "The New

Deal as Raw Deal for Blacks in Segregated Communities," *Washington Post*, May 25, 2017; "African Americans and the New Deal," University of Houston Digital History series; Bartlett, *Wrong on Race*, 113–115.

172. "'I honestly feel...thoroughly worthwhile'": Muder, "President Roosevelt Gives 'Green Light' to Baseball," National Baseball Hall of Fame.

173. "As with any...World War II": Overmyer, *Queen of the Negro Leagues*, 173.

174. "Black baseball...factory jobs": Luke, *Most Famous Woman in Baseball*, 96; letter from Leon Ruffin to Effa Manley, April 15, 1943, Effa Manley Papers, Newark Public Library.

174. "According to Buster Miller...'records kept'": "Time Out," *New York Age*, February 7, 1942.

175. "After each weekday...second secretary": Letter from Ed Gottlieb to NNL owners, May 11, 1939, Effa Manley Papers, Newark Public Library.

176. "'It seems ridiculous...cannot understand'": Letter from Effa to Chester Washington, May 26, 1939, Effa Manley Papers, Newark Public Library.

177. "Abe and Effa...'of his race'": Letter from Effa to Joseph Rainey, December 23, 1941, Effa Manley Papers, Newark Public Library.

177. "Abe didn't...independently": Goldman, "1933–1962: The Business Meetings of Negro League Baseball," Society for American Baseball Research.

178. "When white teams...Major League Baseball": "Are Negro Ball Players Good Enough to 'Crash' the Majors?" *Pittsburgh Courier*, July 15, 22, 29, and August 5, 19, 1939; "Owners Take Notice," *Pittsburgh Courier*, July 15, 1939; Whitaker, *Smoketown*, 235.

179. "In an interview...'was all right'": Dickson, *Leo Durocher: Baseball's Prodigal Son*, 90–91.

180. "Historians question...about integration": Kaiser, David, "A Troubling Myth About Jackie Robinson Endures," Time.com, April 15, 2016; Macht, "Landis and Baseball Before Jackie Robinson: Does Baseball Deserve This Black Eye?" *Baseball Research Journal* 38, no. 1 (Summer 2009).

180. "On May 6...the Majors": Dickson, *Leo Durocher: Baseball's Prodigal Son*, 105–106.

181. "'Certain managers...enforce them'": "Commissioner Landis' Emancipation Proclamation—'Negro Players Are Welcome,'" *Pittsburgh Courier*, July 25, 1942; Pietrusza, *Judge and Jury*, 418.

CHAPTER 18

183. Rickey's baseball experience and early days with the Cardinals: McCue, "Branch Rickey," Society for American Baseball Research; Mann, *Branch Rickey: American in Action*, 87–91, 100–101, 133–135.

185. "As with all...open market": McCue, "Branch Rickey," Society for American Baseball Research.

187. "'[Y]ou should write...young or old'": Mann, *Branch Rickey: American in Action*, 198.

188. Rickey's six-step plan for integration: Mann, *Branch Rickey: American in Action*, 214–215.

188. "During a meeting...'you'll beat it'": Mann, *Branch Rickey: American in Action*, 213.

189. "According to...'forget it'": Polner, *Branch Rickey: A Biography* (revised edition), 134.

190. "On April 6...came of it": Luke, *Most Famous Woman in Baseball*, 115; "Smitty's Sports Spurts," *Pittsburgh Courier*, April 14, 1945.

191. "A week and a half later...spots": Luke, *Most Famous Woman in Baseball*, 115; Whitaker, *Smoketown*, 239–240.

193. "'Let's be extremely careful...big-league standards'": Manley and Hardwick, *Negro Baseball...Before Integration*, 62.

194. "'After much shuttling...then and there'": Manley and Hardwick, *Negro Baseball...Before Integration*, 63.

CHAPTER 19

195. Effa's call with Rickey's secretary: Manley and Hardwick, *Negro Baseball...Before Integration*, 69.

196. "'one of the strangest'...'a lot of things'": Manley and Hardwick, *Negro Baseball...Before Integration*, 69.

197. "It was no surprise...rebuffed as well": McKenna, "Gus Greenlee," Society for American Baseball Research; "Gus Greenlee Organizes New Six-Club League," *Pittsburgh Courier*, January 6, 1945; "Branch Rickey Says He May Be Interested in a Franchise in Sepia League," *Pittsburgh Courier*, April 14, 1945.

198. " 'It is not my purpose... an effective organization' ": "Brooklyn Dodgers Baseball Club Boss Instrumental in Formation of New Baseball League," *New York Age*, May 12, 1945.

199. "He promised... 'all of this' ": Manley and Hardwick, *Negro Baseball... Before Integration*, 70–71; "Brooklyn Dodgers Baseball Club Boss Instrumental in Formation of New Baseball League," *New York Age*, May 12, 1945.

201. "The USL...more established NNL": Manley and Hardwick, *Negro Baseball... Before Integration*, 71.

202. "Shortly after... 'played baseball' ": Mann, *Branch Rickey: American in Action*, 219; Whitaker, *Smoketown*, 241; Holtzman, *No Cheering in the Press Box*, 320.

202. " 'If you like... absolute secrecy' ": Mann, *Branch Rickey: American in Action*, 219–220.

203. "At the end... in his office": Mann, *Branch Rickey: American in Action*, 220.

204. "Effa had... Ebbets Field": Letter from Effa to John Collins of the Brooklyn Dodgers, September 25, 1945, Effa Manley Papers, Newark Public Library; Luke, *Most Famous Woman in Baseball*, 117–118.

205. " 'I have the best'... 'have been having' ": "Dressen's Stars Placed on Spot," *Brooklyn Daily Eagle*, October 5, 1945.

206. "Staying true... unable to commit": Letter from Effa to Satchel Paige, September 13, 1945; letter from Effa to Tom Baird of the Kansas City Monarchs, September 26, 1945; and letter from Baird to Effa, September 29, 1945, Effa Manley Papers, Newark Public Library.

206. "but Effa did add... in a season": Letter from Effa to Sam Lacy, September 29, 1945, Effa Manley Papers, Newark Public Library; Luke, *Most Famous Woman in Baseball*, 118.

206. " 'If my boys'... 'by ten games' ": "Dressen's Stars Placed on Spot," *Brooklyn Daily Eagle*, October 5, 1945.

207. All-Star series Games 1 and 2: "Gregg, Branca Beat Negroes," *New York Daily News*, October 8, 1945.

208. All-Star series Games 3, 4, and 5: "Dressen's Club Too Powerful," *Brooklyn Daily Eagle*, October 15, 1945.

209. "'For the present…Negro National League'": "Dressen's Club Too Powerful," *Brooklyn Daily Eagle*, October 15, 1945.

210. "In a letter…'half the time'": Letter from Effa to Vernon Green, October 20, 1945, Effa Manley Papers, Newark Public Library.

210. "Rickey openly…Dodgers team": Luke, *Most Famous Woman in Baseball*, 119.

210. "Most significantly…Dodgers organization": Mann, *Branch Rickey: American in Action*, 223.

211. "The formal announcement…Black America": "1st Negro in Organized Baseball Signed by Dodgers," *Philadelphia Inquirer*, October 24, 1945; Mann, *Branch Rickey: American in Action*, 224.

211. "'Robinson is the property…remain silent'": "Boro Leaders Support Rickey's Move," *Brooklyn Daily Eagle*, October 25, 1945.

CHAPTER 20

213. "In fact…this way": Mann, *Branch Rickey: American in Action*, 228.

213. "But despite…potential deal": "Monarchs Head Assails Signing," *Philadelphia Inquirer*, October 24, 1945.

214. "In his biography…'payday to payday'": Mann, *Branch Rickey: American in Action*, 220–221.

215. "'The Negro organizations'…Black baseball": Lanctot, *Negro League Baseball*, 279.

216. "'While it is true'…'as we do'": "Majors Can't Act As Outlaws—Griffith," *Boston Globe*, October 25, 1945.

218. "'No one seems…his advantage'": "The Sports Beat," *Pittsburgh Courier*, May 26, 1945.

221. "'Suppose I was…I must'": Robinson, *I Never Had It Made*, 34.

224. "'We feel that…continue to operate'": Letter from Posey to Happy Chandler, November 1, 1945, Effa Manley Papers, Newark Public Library.

225. "'Your two Leagues...give you relief'": Letter from Clark Griffith to Cum Posey, November 5, 1945, Effa Manley Papers, Newark Public Library.

CHAPTER 21

227. "Major League Baseball...baseball's integration": Lanctot, *Negro League Baseball*, 285; Luke, *Most Famous Woman in Baseball*, 121.
228. "The plan...'happy with it'": "Frick Can't See Chandler's Idea of Consolidation," *Austin American*, January 23, 1946.
229. "'I told them...other leagues'": "Chandler Favors Entry of Negro Leagues into Organized Baseball," *Big Spring (TX) Daily Herald*, January 21, 1946.
229. "Chandler's new guidelines...difficult to address": Lanctot, *Negro League Baseball*, 285; Luke, *Most Famous Woman in Baseball*, 121.
231. "On January 29...'a white player'": "Grays Plan Protest of Player Grab," *Pittsburgh Sun-Telegraph*, January 30, 1946; Lanctot, *Negro League Baseball*, 287–288.
232. "In early April...two years prior": Lanctot, *Negro League Baseball*, 288.
233. "'I think'...the Grays": Letter from Effa to Seward Posey, April 8, 1946, Effa Manley Papers, Newark Public Library.
234. "'Anyone under...segregated baseball'": "The Sports Beat," *Pittsburgh Courier*, January 26, 1946.

CHAPTER 22

237. "Irvin joined...ever since": Hogan, "Monte Irvin," Society for American Baseball Research.
238. "Just a few days...'for ourselves'": Luke, *Most Famous Woman in Baseball*, 86–87.
239. "'If it had been'...she added": Letter from Effa to Art Carter, March 4, 1942, Effa Manley Papers, Newark Public Library.
240. "'I believe...right move'": Letter from Effa to Monte Irvin, February 9, 1946, Effa Manley Papers, Newark Public Library.
241. Eagles' May 5, 1946, game: "Day Beats Stars in No-Hitter, 2-0,"

Philadelphia Inquirer, May 6, 1946; Bush and Nowlin, *Newark Eagles Take Flight*, ebook, chap. 34.

243. "'It was ... thrill that was'": Letter from Effa to Art Carter, May 9, 1946, Effa Manley Papers, Newark Public Library.

243. Recap of the Eagles' 1946 regular season: Bush and Nowlin, *Newark Eagles Take Flight*, ebook, chap. 33.

245. Game 1 of the Negro World Series: "Monarchs Top Newark in Negro Series Tilt," *Baltimore Sun*, September 18, 1946; Bush and Nowlin, *Newark Eagles Take Flight*, ebook, chap. 38, loc. 14443.

245. Game 2 of the Negro World Series: "Newark Eagles Win, Even Negro Series," *Baltimore Sun*, September 20, 1946; Luke, *Most Famous Woman in Baseball*, 128–129; Bush and Nowlin, *Newark Eagles Take Flight*, ebook, chap. 38, loc. 14488–14540.

246. Games 3, 4, and 5 of the Negro World Series: Luke, *Most Famous Woman in Baseball*, 129; Bush and Nowlin, *Newark Eagles Take Flight*, ebook, chap. 38, loc. 14540–14690.

247. Game 6 of the Negro World Series: "Eagles Beat Monarchs, Square Negro Series," *News Journal* (Wilmington, DE), September 28, 1946; Luke, *Most Famous Woman in Baseball*, 129; Bush and Nowlin, *Newark Eagles Take Flight*, ebook, chap. 38, loc. 14691–14740.

CHAPTER 23

248. "It was ... slightly humid": Manley and Hardwick, *Negro Baseball ... Before Integration*, 35.

249. "Notably ... Cleveland Indians": Bush and Nowlin, *Newark Eagles Take Flight*, ebook, chap. 38, loc. 14752.

249. Game 7 of the Negro World Series: Manley and Hardwick, *Negro Baseball ... Before Integration*, 36–37; Luke, *Most Famous Woman in Baseball*, 129–130; Overmyer, *Queen of the Negro Leagues*, 207; Bush and Nowlin, *Newark Eagles Take Flight*, ebook, chap. 38, loc. 14788–14807.

CHAPTER 24

254. "He'd become...that fall": Jackie Robinson, Baseball-reference.com.

254. Jackie Robinson's first game with the Dodgers: Spatz, "1947 Dodgers: Jackie Robinson's first game," Society for American Baseball Research.

256. "but according...he was terrible": Robinson, *I Never Had It Made*, 58.

256. "Johnny Wright...New York": "Branch Rickey Jr. Gives Montreal the Once-Over," *Pittsburgh Courier*, May 25, 1946; "Forgotten members of the 'great experiment,'" Milb.com, February 13, 2007; Roy Partlow career stats, seamheads.com; "The Sports Beat/What Happened to Roy Partlow?" *Pittsburgh Courier*, July 20, 1946.

258. "'[Partlow] should...his position'": "The Sports Beat/What Happened to Roy Partlow?" *Pittsburgh Courier*, July 20, 1946.

259. "Jackie Robinson...29 stolen bases": "Robinson Debuts Five Days After Signing With Dodgers," Baseballhall.org.

259. "'Money is America's God...'Noble Experiment'''": Robinson, *I Never Had It Made*, xx.

261. "'[Black fans]...never happened'": Robinson, *I Never Had It Made*, xxi.

261. "Due in part...that year": Eig, *Opening Day*, 231.

262. "Overnight, it seemed...for a game": Manley and Hardwick, *Negro Baseball...Before Integration*, 93–94.

CHAPTER 25

264. "Few knew it...for his team": Tygiel, "Revisiting Bill Veeck and the 1943 Phillies," *Baseball Research Journal* 35 (2006), 113–114.

265. "'Out of my...unthinkable'": Veeck, *Veeck as in Wreck*, 171.

267. "Effa was enjoying...'buying him'": Manley and Hardwick, *Negro Baseball...Before Integration*, 74.

268. Effa's call with Bill Veeck: Manley and Hardwick, *Negro Baseball...Before Integration*, 74–77; interview with Effa Manley, Louie B. Nunn Center for Oral History, University of Kentucky Libraries, 1:50:21.

271. "Doby played...historic nonetheless": McMurray, "Larry Doby," Society for American Baseball Research.

CHAPTER 26

273. "'There was little...Major League club'": Manley and Hardwick, *Negro Baseball...Before Integration*, 95.

273. "Still, the '47 season...Max Manning": Overmyer, *Queen of the Negro Leagues*, 239–240.

274. "After drawing...12,552": "Dan Parker Broadway Bugle," *Courier-Post* (Camden, NJ), January 6, 1948.

274. "'If more people...creditable year'": Overmyer, *Queen of the Negro Leagues*, 240.

276. "'It is more important...anyway'": "The Sports Beat," *Pittsburgh Courier*, May 3, 1947.

276. "He had long stopped...glory days": Lanctot, *Negro League Baseball*, 330–331.

277. "'The year 1948...box office'": Manley and Hardwick, *Negro Baseball...Before Integration*, 95.

277. "Smith, unsurprisingly...Black baseball": "The Sports Beat," *Pittsburgh Courier*, September 20, 1947.

278. "'My five short months...team owners'": "What's Wrong with Negro Baseball?" *Ebony* magazine, June 1948, 16–19.

279. "in his autobiography...'financial bonanza'": Robinson, *I Never Had It Made*, 23.

279. "'Today...had it made'": Robinson, *I Never Had It Made*, xxii.

280. "'I charge...he derides'": "Mrs. Effa Manley Says Eagles Got $15,000 for Doby," *Morning Call* (Paterson, NJ), May 22, 1948.

280. "according to Effa...Ruppert Stadium": Manley and Hardwick, *Negro Baseball...Before Integration*, 95–96.

281. "'Effa Manley...tears and all'": "The Sports Beat/Baseball's Glamour Girl Bows Out," *Pittsburgh Courier*, September 18, 1948.

283. "'Baseball is...two years'": "Effa Blasts Fans, Press for NNL Flop," *New York Age*, September 21, 1948.

CHAPTER 27

284. "With the Eagles ... 1949 season": Overmyer, *Queen of the Negro Leagues*, 240–241.

285. "The reinforced ... the Manleys": Overmyer, *Queen of the Negro Leagues*, 241; Manley and Hardwick, *Negro Baseball ... Before Integration*, 89–90.

285. "Like the rest ... 'to play'": Manley and Hardwick, *Negro Baseball ... Before Integration*, 89–90.

286. "'Abe and I' ... her memoir": Manley and Hardwick, *Negro Baseball ... Before Integration*, 90.

286. "Rickey replied ... promptly released": "Will Free Irvin If Signing Illegal," *Berkshire Eagle* (Pittsfield, MA), January 13, 1949.

287. "'The Giants ... precedent setter'": Manley and Hardwick, *Negro Baseball ... Before Integration*, 91.

289. "'Abe agreed ... small role'": Manley and Hardwick, *Negro Baseball ... Before Integration*, 92.

BIBLIOGRAPHY

BOOKS AND PAPERS

Bartlett, Bruce. *Wrong on Race: The Democratic Party's Buried Past.* New York: Palgrave Macmillan, 2008.

Bascom, Lionel C., ed. *A Renaissance in Harlem: The Lost Voices of an American Community.* New York: Avon/HarperCollins, 1999.

Bush, Frederick C., and Bill Nowlin, eds. *The Newark Eagles Take Flight: The Story of the 1946 Negro League Champions.* Phoenix: SABR, 2019.

Cottrell, Robert Charles. *The Best Pitcher in Baseball: The Life of Rube Foster, Negro League Giant.* New York: New York University Press, 2001.

Dickson, Paul. *Leo Durocher: Baseball's Prodigal Son.* New York: Bloomsbury, 2017.

Economic Consequences of War on the US Economy. (Sydney: Institute for Economics and Peace, 2011). http://economicsandpeace.org/wp-content/uploads/2015/06/The-Economic-Consequences-of-War-on-US-Economy_0.pdf.

Eig, Jonathan. *Opening Day: The Story of Jackie Robinson's First Season.* New York: Simon & Schuster, 2007.

Harris, LaShawn. "Playing the Numbers: Madame Stephanie St. Clair and African American Policy Culture in Harlem." *Black Women, Gender and Families,* University of Illinois Press, 2, no. 2 (Fall 2008): 53–76.

Heaphy, Leslie A. *The Negro Leagues: 1869–1960.* Jefferson, NC: McFarland, 2003.

Holtzman, Jerome. *No Cheering in the Press Box* (first revised edition). New York: Henry Holt, 1995.

Holway, John. *Black Diamonds: Life in the Negro Leagues from the Men Who Lived It.* Westport, CT: Meckler Books, 1990.

Lanctot, Neil. *Negro League Baseball: The Rise and Ruin of a Black Institution.* Philadelphia: University of Pennsylvania Press, 2004.

Lester, Larry. *Rube Foster in His Time.* Jefferson, NC: McFarland, 2012.

Lewis, David Levering. *W. E. B. Du Bois: The Fight for Equality and the American Century, 1919–1963*. New York: Henry Holt, 2000.

Luke, Bob. *The Most Famous Woman in Baseball: Effa Manley and the Negro Leagues*. Washington, DC: Potomac Books, 2011.

Macht, Norman L. "Landis and Baseball Before Jackie Robinson: Does Baseball Deserve This Black Eye?" *Baseball Research Journal* 38, no. 1 (Summer 2009). https://sabr.org/content/baseball-research-journal-archives.

Manley, Effa, and Leon Hardwick. *Negro Baseball . . . Before Integration*. Chicago: Adams, 1976.

Mann, Arthur. *Branch Rickey: American in Action*. Boston, MA: Houghton Mifflin, 1957.

Newman, Roberta J., and Joel Nathan Rosen. *Black Baseball Black Business: Race Enterprise and the Fate of the Segregated Dollar*. Jackson: University Press of Mississippi, 2014.

Overmyer, James. *Queen of the Negro Leagues: Effa Manley and the Newark Eagles*. Metuchen, NJ: Scarecrow Press, 1993.

Pietrusza, David. *Judge and Jury: The Life and Times of Judge Kenesaw Mountain Landis*. South Bend, IN: Diamond Communications, 1998.

Polner, Murray. *Branch Rickey: A Biography* (revised edition). New York: Atheneum, 1982.

Revel, Layton. "Early Pioneers of the Negro Leagues: Nat Strong." Center for Negro League Baseball Research. http://www.cnlbr.org/Portals/0/EP/Nat%20Strong%202018-04.pdf.

Revel, Layton, and Luis Munoz. "Early Pioneers of the Negro Leagues: Frank C. Leland." Center for Negro League Baseball Research. http://www.cnlbr.org/Portals/0/EP/332567%20Forgotten%20Heroes%20Frank%20C%20Leland%20Single%20Pages.pdf.

Riley, James A. *The Biographical Encyclopedia of the Negro Baseball Leagues*. New York: Carroll & Graf, 1994.

Robinson, Jackie. *I Never Had It Made: The Autobiography of Jackie Robinson*. New York: Putnam, 1972.

Saint-Arnaud, Pierre, and Peter Feldstein. *African American Pioneers of Sociology: A Critical History*. Toronto: University of Toronto Press, 2009.

Sclar, Ari, ed. *Beyond Stereotypes: American Jews and Sports in the Twentieth Century.* West Lafayette, IN: Purdue University Press, 2014.

Swanson, Ryan A. *When Baseball Went White: Reconstruction, Reconciliation, and Dreams of a National Pastime.* Lincoln: Board of Regents of the University of Nebraska, 2014.

Tye, Larry. *Satchel: The Life and Times of an American Legend.* New York: Random House, 2009.

Tygiel, Jules. "Revisiting Bill Veeck and the 1943 Phillies." *Baseball Research Journal* 35 (2006). http://research.sabr.org/journals/files/SABR-Baseball _Research_Journal-35.pdf.

Veeck, Bill. *Veeck as in Wreck.* Chicago: University of Chicago Press, 2001.

Whitaker, Mark. *Smoketown: The Untold Story of the Other Great Black Renaissance.* New York: Simon & Schuster, 2018.

NEWSPAPERS AND MAGAZINES

Austin American

Baltimore Sun

Baseballhall.org (National Baseball Hall of Fame)

Berkshire Eagle (Pittsfield, MA)

Big Spring (TX) Daily Herald

Boston Globe

Brooklyn Daily Eagle

Buffalo (NY) Commercial

Chicago Defender

Courier-Post (Camden, NJ)

Ebony magazine

ESPN.com

Inter Ocean (Chicago)

Milb.com

Morning Call (Paterson, NJ)

New York Age

New York Daily News

New York Times
News Journal (Wilmington, DE)
New-York Tribune
Philadelphia Inquirer
Pittsburgh Courier
Pittsburgh Press
Pittsburgh Sun-Telegraph
Survey Graphic magazine
Time.com
Times Union (Brooklyn, NY)
Washington Post
Washington Times
Windsor (ON) Star

WEBSITES, ONLINE ARTICLES, AND OTHER SOURCES

Baseball Reference, baseballreference.com

Effa Manley Papers, Newark Public Library

Negro Leagues Database, seamheads.com

Society for American Baseball Research, sabr.org

"African Americans and the New Deal." University of Houston Digital History series. digitalhistory.uh.edu/disp_textbook.cfm?smtID=2&psid =3447.

Black Perspectives (blog). African American Intellectual History Society. aaihs.org/black-perspectives/.

"Booker T. Washington Delivers the 1895 Atlanta Compromise Speech." History Matters: The US Survey Course on the Web. historymatters.gmu.edu/d/39/.

Du Bois, W. E. B. "The Talented Tenth." moses.law.umn.edu/darrow /documents/Talented_Tenth.pdf.

"Fantasy Baseball: The Momentous Drawing of the Sport's 19th Century 'Color Line' Is Still Tripping Up History Writers." howardwrosenberg .atavist.com/racism-bbhistory.

Manley, Effa, interview by William J. Marshall, October 19, 1977, A. B. "Happy" Chandler: Desegregation of Major League Baseball Oral History Project, Louie B. Nunn Center for Oral History, University of Kentucky Libraries. kentuckyoralhistory.org/ark:/16417 /xt798s4jnv7d.

"Marcus Garvey." The Official Website of the Universal Negro Improvement Association and African Communities League. theunia-acl.com /index.php/history/marcus-garvey.

Muder, Craig. "President Roosevelt Gives 'Green Light' to Baseball." National Baseball Hall of Fame. baseballhall.org/discover /inside-pitch/roosevelt-sendsgreen-light-letter.

PHOTO CREDITS

Page 2: National Baseball Hall of Fame Library; 21: public domain; 23: National Portrait Gallery, Smithsonian Institution; 33: Chicago History Museum/ Getty Images; 38: Everett Collection Inc/Alamy Stock Photo; 46: National Baseball Hall of Fame Library; 49: Negro Leagues Baseball Museum, Inc.; 55: Jack Delano/Library of Congress; 57: C. M. Battey/Library of Congress, George Grantham Bain Collection/Library of Congress; 62, 66, 77: National Baseball Hall of Fame Library; 81: Negro Leagues Baseball Museum, Inc; 86: Archive Photos/Getty Images; 94: Office for Metropolitan History; 98: National Baseball Hall of Fame Library; 105: Negro Leagues Baseball Museum, Inc.; 107, 116, 119: National Baseball Hall of Fame Library; 122: Newark Public Library; 126, 133: National Baseball Hall of Fame Library; 135: Negro Leagues Baseball Museum, Inc.; 145: National Baseball Hall of Fame Library; 152: Mark Rucker/ Transcendental Graphics, Getty Images; 157: Library of Congress; 162: National Baseball Hall of Fame Library; 163: Associated Press; 171: United States National Recovery Administration/Library of Congress; 179: Photo by Charles 'Teenie' Harris/Carnegie Museum of Art/Getty Images; 184: National Photo Company Collection/Library of Congress; 191: Negro Leagues Baseball Museum, Inc; 199: *New York Times* via Pars International; 203: National Baseball Hall of Fame Library; 205: Newark Public Library; 214: Meyer Liebowitz/*New York Times*/ Redux; 216: National Photo Company Collection/Library of Congress; 228: Marie Hansen/The LIFE Picture Collection via Getty Images; 232: Negro Leagues Baseball Museum, Inc; 241: Newark Public Library; 244: National Baseball Hall of Fame Library; 252: *Pittsburgh Courier* archives; 255: Bettman/Getty Images; 257: National Baseball Hall of Fame Library; 270: Sporting News via Getty Images; 272: National Baseball Hall of Fame Library; 281: *Pittsburgh Courier* archives; 287: National Baseball Hall of Fame Library; 289: Mark Rucker/ Transcendental Graphics, Getty Images

INDEX

Walker, Moses Fleetwood, *21*, 21–22, 28, 30–32, 53, 187
Washington, Booker T., 52, 53, 56, 299n4
Washington, Chester, 176
Washington Senators, 216, 219
Washington Times, 51
wealth, of Manley, A., 82
Weiss, George, 130, 131
Wells, Willie, 132
WGN (radio network), 156
White, Sol, 28
white suffragists, 14
Wilkes, Jimmy, 250
Wilkinson, J. L., 212, 215, 233
Williams, Marvin, 191–92
Williams, Ted, 291

Wilson, Tom, 145, 161, 164, 177, 227, 274
winter baseball leagues, 126–27
women, 14, 93–94
  dark-skinned, 96
  domestics, 86
  employment of, 86–90
World Series, 184
World War I, 103
World War II, 159, 167, 170, 171–72, 174, 237
Wright, Johnny, 209, 210, 231, 233, 256, 257, 259

Yankee Stadium, 161, *162*, 164
Young, Fay, 265
Young, W. H., 285, 288

330